W9-BWD-113

UFOs FOR THE MILLIONS

UFOs FOR THE MILLIONS

by Howard V. Chambers

Bell Publishing Company, Inc. · New York

Library of Congress Catalog Card Number 67-15082

Manufactured in the United States of America

This edition published by Bell Publishing Company, Inc.,
a division of Crown Publishers, Inc., by
arrangement with Sherbourne Press, Inc.
A B C D E F G H

The author wishes to extend special thanks to the Santa Monica, Calif. library for sympathetic and extensive help, and to Miss Kathy Robin for an abundance of useful and intriguing research assistance.

Contents

CHAPTER ONE

Introduction

For Kenneth Arnold, a thirty-two-year-old businessman from Boise, Idaho, the afternoon of June 24, 1947 was already out of the ordinary. Because he was flying his private plane between Chehalis and Yakima, Washington, he had been asked to search the valleys and peaks around Mount Rainier for the wreckage of a missing C-54 Marine transport.

Arnold did not see the wreckage, but at approximately three o'clock on the bright, clear afternoon, he saw a tiger which he promptly handed over to the U.S. Air Force. The Air Force has held that tiger—rather uncomfortably—by the tail ever since and now, nearly twenty years later, is more than willing to pay $300,000, with more to come, for help.

Arnold's "tiger" was a formation of nine "very bright, disc-shaped objects," each of which he estimated to be 45 to 50 feet in length. They sped past the nose of his airplane at a speed he estimated as 1700 miles per hour, weaved in and out of mountain peaks with great mobility, then summarily disappeared.

Although reports of such sightings throughout the ages are numerous, Arnold's encounter with the flying discs is considered a classic and the beginning of the modern era of flying saucers. The term "classic" is given to this sighting and a few others which are closely grouped in time for several reasons:

These sightings were responsible for official motivation by the Air Technical Intelligence Center (ATIC) of the Air Force to set up Project Bluebook, a high-priority, high-security investigation of subsequent flying saucer reports.

They were responsible for waves of rumors, panic, and fantastic reports, the mildest of which was that earth is now being watched by alien beings from other worlds, the strongest of which held that these alien beings were of hostile intent.

They were responsible for the coining of the term UFO (Unidentified Flying Object) by ATIC chief, Edward J. Ruppelt.

They caused to be established a firm set of standards against which most subsequent UFO reports were judged.

They were instrumental in causing the eventual admission by ATIC, however tacit and indirect at times, that many UFOs were solid machines, not illusions, and that they probably are of an origin alien to this world because they do not conform to the appearance or the performance capabilities of any known aircraft.

All these conclusions of alien craft and alien surveillance were hard won and subject to frequent contradiction and, even more, explanation as natural phenomena. But as the ATIC's files grew thicker with the reports of more sightings, it had to admit that many instances could not be fobbed off as hallucinations, balloons, cloud formations, or atmospheric freaks.

And even if every case previous to the 1947 classics is written off, still there is a startling statement which must stand. During the course of the past twenty years, there have been significant UFO sightings over every major European city, over every major American city, over major military installations throughout Asia and Europe, and over every major American Strategic Air Command and nuclear installation.

These sightings have been made by trained radar technicians, by experienced military and civilian pilots, by astronomers, and by scientists in other disciplines. We have records which show a locking in of UFO position on more than one radar screen and subsequent eye-witness reports and radar contact records made by Air Force jets which were sent to give pursuit.

The most determined and professional interrogation has not been able to "shake" such reports, and it is understating the case to say that hundreds of these authenticated reports were made by men who could certainly tell the difference between such illusions as weather inversions, cloud formations, balloons, and a solid object—a UFO. And even if we were to arbitrarily discard 80 per cent of all UFO sightings since 1947 we would still be left with a considerable number of reliable, documented reports that UFOs are solid, highly maneuverable machines, capable of hovering at will or moving at thousands of miles an hour.

In the past twenty years, a growing number of people have come forward with claims that they have seen flying saucers at close hand, have been inside them, ridden in them, and had contact with the humanlike beings who piloted them. If we apply to these instances the same, arbitrary rule of discounting 80 per cent of the cases, we still have a number of people who are unshaken in their belief that the experiences they had were real.

Unofficial investigation groups, tired of the skeptical approach of many scientists and impatient with the caution of the Air Force, have begun compiling their own records of sightings and incidents. Such groups are more likely to attract less objective points of view, but they have also attracted competent people of good character. Even if we discard *all* findings of these unofficial groups, we cannot state positively that UFOs are merely an illusion.

Always cyclic in nature, new UFO sightings are once again on the upswing. Air Force figures show a swing from 399 officially reported sightings in 1963 to over 1500 in the period from mid-1965 to the end of 1966.

From the information we now have available to us, it is safer to conclude that UFOs are real than to attempt disproving them. Although this book cannot prove the existence of flying saucers, it can and will present the UFO story in terms of the material we have available today and discuss what use has been made of that information. We will infer that UFOs are real on the premise that not to do so would be similar to burying our heads in the sand.

We will attempt to lay the groundwork here for understanding UFO phenomena in terms of new discoveries which may come. In this groundwork is one recent fact of great significance. In efforts to get other hands on the tail of the tiger it is holding, the Air Force recently awarded the University of Colorado a $300,000 budget to undertake an eighteen-month study of flying saucers. This could merely mean the Air Force is overly sensitive to a recent Gallup Poll showing over five million persons in America as believers that UFOs are real. But it could also mean the Air Force wants a fresh point of view, more conclusions which might agree with its own, and an end to rumors and inferences that it is "holding something back" from the American people. It could also mean that the Air Force is convinced that something is really there when the reputable sighters say so.

This book will discuss the sightings, the persons who made them, the persons who made evaluations of the sightings, and what people who think they've made actual contacts with aliens think these sightings mean. Several writers, authorities, and agencies have already presented to us the proposition that UFOs are no longer things we can ignore. Our purpose here is to consider some of these things we cannot ignore and, if possible, discover why.

CHAPTER TWO

The Modern Classics

While Edward J. Ruppelt, chief of ATIC's Project Bluebook, was investigating the Kenneth Arnold UFO sighting, he had the good fortune to meet a fighter-bomber pilot who actually knew the young civilian. This pilot turned out to be an extremely good lead for Ruppelt. Not only was he a former newspaper reporter who, in civilian life, had actually covered the Arnold sighting, he was, as well, a long-time resident of the Pacific Northwest and had logged hundreds of hours of flying time in the area. In addition to solidifying Ruppelt's belief that Arnold had an excellent reputation and was not someone likely to perpetrate such a hoax, the pilot said, "Personally, I believe Arnold saw some kind of aircraft and they weren't from this earth."

The pilot's opinion was shared by many, and between that afternoon in late June, when the first "classic" sighting was made, and the end of the year there were literally hundreds of additional sightings. Many of these were written off as unreliable, but the remaining reports were carefully categorized by Project Bluebook as unexplainable, as good a way as any of saying something was there, but the Air Force didn't care to say what.

The "acceptable" reports in the final months of 1947 were

from such unimpeachable sources that the press and the public began to have a field day. Controversy flared. Authorities wanted to write off all UFO sightings as balloons, atmospheric conditions, and the reflections of light on the bottoms of clouds. But the public would have none of it. Newspapermen openly wondered how it was that trained radar observers, Air Force pilots, and the pilots flying for commercial airlines were suddenly supposed to be fatigued or hallucinating when they made their UFO reports? Why hadn't these men been relieved of duty if they were so tired?

Unaccountably, flying saucer reports trailed off, but interest in UFOs still ran high, so high that a new report truly had to be unique and well authenticated before any great importance could be attached to it. Kenneth Arnold's run-in with his flying saucers was still the best look, the most reliable report that had been had to date. But not for long. On January 7, 1948, the Mantell Incident made the list of "classics" and eclipsed the Arnold sighting in excitement and tragedy.

The time was one-fifteen in the afternoon. The place: Godman Air Force Base, just outside of Louisville, Kent. Control tower personnel received a call from the State Highway Patrol; did Godman tower know anything about strange aircraft hovering in the vicinity? The Godman tower replied in the negative. Nothing airborne in the vicinity. As a check, they called Flight Service at the Wright-Patterson Air Force Base. Still no response or record of anything in the area.

State Highway Patrol reluctantly concluded there was nothing more they could do about calls they'd had from Maysville, a small town 80 miles east of Louisville. But twenty minutes later, they were back on the phone to Godman tower with reports from two towns west of Louisville. The reports from each town seemed to jibe. A flat, circular object, about

13

300 feet in diameter, was moving westward at an appreciable rate of speed. Although they'd been looking since the first report, Godman tower still saw nothing. They checked Wright-Patterson again and got another negative response.

Then, at 1:45 P.M., it happened. The assistant tower operator saw the object for several minutes before reporting it to the chief. Both men tried to convince themselves the object was a balloon but could not. Key personnel were alerted to the tower where they all viewed the object through 6 × 50 binoculars. None could identify the object, but all saw it. Then the base commander arrived and he, too, saw the object.

At two-thirty, a flight of four F-51's hove into view, and the base commander made up his mind. He called Captain Mantell, the flight leader, and asked him to identify the object. Neither Mantell nor the three other pilots could see the object. After one of the F-51's dropped out of the flight because his fuel level was low, the three remaining aircraft took a heading from Godman tower and headed south.

By the time the F-51's reached 10,000 feet, Mantell was well ahead of his wing men and barely visible to them. He called into the tower. "I see something ahead of me and I'm still climbing." Everyone in the tower heard this. They also heard one of the wing men say, "What the hell are we looking for?"

Godman tower called Mantell now for a description. To this day, there is controversy over most of what he told them. Yet they do agree on one thing. "It's above me and I'm gaining on it. I'm going to 20,000 feet."

None of the pilots had oxygen, and Mantell's announcement that he was climbing to 20,000 feet meant immediate trouble. Twelve thousand feet is an altitude where oxygen is definitely indicated, at 15,000 feet and over, it is essential. His two wing men tried desperately to call Mantell, but he did not answer. They leveled off at 15,000 feet, made other efforts to call their leader, then started down, their own fuel dangerously low.

The two remaining aircraft returned to their base, and at 3:50 Godman tower lost sight of the UFO. Minutes later, the report came in that Mantell's plane had crashed; he was dead. Later that evening, airfields throughout the Midwest sent in UFO reports, and newspapers carrying the story of the Mantell tragedy linked the subsequent sightings with the Kentucky sightings, claiming it was one object and that it had led Mantell to his death.

Rumor and controversy sprang up immediately. Some sources hinted that because the Air Force had refused to release pictures of Mantell's body, this was proof that he had been burned by radiation, had been atomized, and had been magnetized. The Air Force said they never released such pictures out of respect to the deceased individual's survivors.

The Air Force also said Mantell had not, in fact, seen a flying saucer but that he had been chasing the planet Venus, which was in sight that afternoon, at the precise direction in which Mantell had been flying. The Air Force added that it was possible that the UFO had been a balloon. Subsequent investigations tended to discredit the Venus theory as too extraordinary and Air Force spokesmen said the balloon theory was a possible one because a balloon had been released in the area that day and could have been seen by Mantell.

But there were still unanswered questions. Why would Mantell, an experienced pilot, risk 20,000 feet without an oxygen mask? Did he, as some of the Godman tower personnel insisted, say he was seeing an object that was "metallic and . . . tremendous in size?" Did he, in fact, see something

15

he may have thought was more important to him than his life? The facts of Mantell's death have very few specifics. Among them are the probabilities that he blacked out at 20,000 feet, went into a dive, and lost a wing because of excessive speed.

The Mantell case is tantalizing. We may dismiss it completely if we buy the explanation possibilities that a trained pilot was chasing a balloon or a planet. Either of these would leave no untidy loose ends. But as it stands now, the Mantell case is still open and unclassified, the first casualty on the modern list of classic sightings.

On July 24, 1948, Captain C. S. Chiles and First Officer John B. Whitted were convinced their Eastern Air Lines flight from Houston to Atlanta was routine. They continued thinking so until 2:45 A.M., when the position of their DC-3 was 20 miles southwest of Montgomery, Ala. It was then Capt. Chiles saw a light dead ahead, closing on the DC-3 fast, so fast that Chiles almost immediately cast aside any possibility that the approaching light was a jet aircraft.

First Officer Whitted saw the object too. Both men agreed it was a brilliant, cigar-shaped craft. "It flashed toward us at terrific speed," Chiles said. With the UFO dangerously close and on a collision course, Chiles fought the DC-3 into a tight left turn. Both men saw the UFO veer away. "It veered sharply, too, and passed us about 700 feet to the right."

Chiles and Whitted got a good look at the cigar-shaped craft and passed along to the ATIC a description of "two rows of windows from which bright blue lights glowed." The UFO left a 50-foot trail of orange-red flame. Speed of the object was estimated by both men as between 500 and 700 miles per hour. As it raced past the DC-3, pulling up sharply, a propulsion blast rocked the slower ship.

What was probably the same object was sighted minutes

later over Robbins Field, near Macon, Ga. It was described by viewers as an extremely bright light, passing overhead at tremendous speed. Another pilot, in flight near the Virginia–North Carolina border, made a report of seeing a bright shooting star that night.

The reports, times, and estimated speeds from these three sightings all jibed and there can be little doubt that all three sources saw the same UFO—whatever it was.

On October 1, 1948, another UFO incident made headlines and history when George Gorman, a twenty-five-year-old second-lieutenant in the North Dakota Air National Guard returned to Fargo, N.D., on the last leg of a cross-country flight. After flying over the field, Gorman called in for permission and landing instructions. He was told his clearance would be forthcoming after a Piper Cub (a small, single-engine private plane) which was in the area and was ordered to extend his approach accordingly.

Everything was fine, so far. But then, Gorman was passed on his immediate right by what he took to be the tail light of another aircraft. Gorman called the Fargo tower and complained that their negligence could have given him trouble. The tower replied tersely. The Piper Cub was the only aircraft in the vicinity except for Gorman.

By this time, Gorman's temper flared. He saw the light again, regardless of what the tower said. He nosed into a tight turn and gave chase to the light. As he turned, he could see the Piper Cub, clearly outlined against the lights of the city. Ahead of him was the bright light, which was not outlined at all.

Gorman closed the gap to an estimated 1,000 yards of the mysterious light and got quite a surprise. He saw the light now, a sharply outlined disc which was about 8 inches in diameter, blinking on and off, more or less pulsating. Then the pulsing light became steady as the disc put on more power and cut into a sharp left turn.

There followed what can best be called a dogfight; Gorman and the disc made several passes at each other, with Gorman attempting to get a closer look, the disc cleverly evading him.

After preliminary parrying, the disc headed directly at Gorman, apparently on a direct collision course. At the last minute, Gorman was able to maneuver away by making a sharp dive. The flying saucer skimmed rapidly over his cockpit, made a steep bank, then closed at Gorman again, head on. And for the second time, the young lieutenant had to dive to avoid collision. After this pass, the flying disc seemed to lose interest in the chase. It rose rapidly and moved out of sight, easily outdistancing Gorman's attempts at pursuit.

Later, partial corroboration of Gorman's sighting was given by the pilot of the Piper Cub, a Fargo oculist. On the ground, two Civil Aeronautics Administration personnel had seen the saucer's light flashing over the field as Gorman chased it, but neither the oculist nor the CAA men saw all the details of the dogfight Gorman reported. When he made his report to ATIC, Gorman said he was sure the disc had been "controlled by thought or reason."

These are the UFO modern classics. They have had copious exposure in books, newspapers, magazines, and government reports. Even in such cases as Donald H. Menzel's controversial *World of Flying Saucers*, where the author's intent was not only skeptical but negative, these classics appear. They are the framework on which modern UFO opinions are built. And each one of them had a spectacular, if different, effect on the Air Force and on the public.

Kenneth Arnold's sighting brought new authority to UFO

reports and helped christen UFOs as flying saucers. Although several descriptions of previous sightings had used the words "saucerlike" or "saucer-shaped," it was Arnold's use of these terms that found their way into newspaper accounts as flying saucers.

The Mantell affair resulted in a tragic death and rumors that he had been deliberately subjected to a fatal laser beam by the UFO he was chasing.

The Chiles–Whitted sighting over Montgomery had additional confirmations over an area so large that it seemed to confirm the belief that UFOs, because of their tremendous speed, surely were not of this earth.

The Gorman incident served two important functions. It gave many persons the uncomfortable notion that flying saucers might possibly have a hostile intent. Then there was the matter of Gorman's description of his saucer, a brightly flashing disc of about 8 inches in diameter. The moment this description was made public, the ATIC was besieged with new speculations and reminiscences of the famous foo planes.

CHAPTER THREE

More about Modern UFOs

Reports of Lt. Gorman's 8-inch brightly lit disc rekindled interest in a baffling phenomenon frequently reported by fliers in World War II and led ATIC into a curious investigation. In subsequent months, ATIC found itself with a thick dossier of reports similar to Gorman's.

In every major theater of operation, World War II pilots had reported sightings of shining discs, from 6 to 8 inches in diameter. These discs often seemed to hover at the sight of air battles or extensive air operations, as though they were watching the outcome. Many pilots passed over these discs or stories about them, relating them to the famed gremlins, those imaginary little beings which supposedly teased, plagued, and tormented pilots. "We even had them [gremlins] in Korea," a photo reconnaissance pilot said. "Although I never saw one, it was still a popular myth. If anything went wrong with your aircraft, or if you forgot to perform some vital operation, you blamed it on the gremlins."

Yet reports of these flying discs persisted, and in some cases the discs were described as having made passes at our aircraft, narrowly avoiding collision. This sort of reporting quickly extended itself, and at one time the Air Force entertained the notion that these small discs were new weapons being used by the Germans and the Japanese.

ATIC went into action and began questioning Japanese and German pilots, only to learn that they, too, had had the same experiences with the foo planes. Both the Japanese and Germans, although they had different names for the foo planes, thought they were of American or British origin! We'll have to accept on faith the fact that someone began calling these small discs foo planes. We do know that the Japanese called them devil discs, and the Germans had a name which could translate out roughly as flying saucers.

These foo planes belong to one of four categories of saucers we know about in sightings authenticated to the end of 1966. Lt. Gorman's belief that they were operated by thought or reason seems to hold up. Certainly too small to permit any kind of intelligent life as a pilot or passenger, these foo planes are best described as reconnaissance and sighting discs, released from and controlled by larger UFOs. Like many of the other UFOs on report, these foo discs apparently change color when they change speed. They are, as we have seen in the Gorman incident, capable of great speeds and high maneuverability. Apparently they are either photo or light sensitive, possibly both, since they seem always to be able to detect the presence of oncoming aircraft.

Sightings of the foo discs over such areas as Seattle, White Sands, N.M., the George Air Force Base near Victorville, Calif., and Buffalo, N.Y., could be linked to other accounts of explosions in the sky, some of which have been observed at relatively close quarters. If we rule out the possibility of such astronomical phenomena as shooting stars and meteorites, we approach the growing conclusion that the foo discs are, in fact, unmanned scouting and survey craft which occasionally run into mechanical difficulties and destroy themselves or are destroyed on command from the mother ship.

This theory is not as tenuous as it may seem. Detractors of it point out that nearly all UFOs sighted at night appear to give off intense lights, sometimes blue, sometimes white, but also yellow and red. And the great majority of sighting reports agree that all UFOs appear to change colors before acceleration, while hovering, or while reducing speed. Since UFOs are capable of great speeds, they say, doesn't it follow that many reports of "explosions" are merely optical illusions resulting from changing colors spread over a great area?

Detractors also ask how it is that no scraps or fragments from these alleged explosions have ever been recovered. The answer is that we simply do not know. But we do know that air and ground observations of alleged explosion phenomena suggest a diffusion of brightly lit particles in a pattern that greatly suggests what we think of as an explosion.

The theory must rest there until more definite proof arises. Meanwhile, considering the successes we have had with some of our own unmanned space capsules and data-gathering satellites, we have the probability of the small, highly mobile foo discs as individual information collecting craft which beam their findings back to a mother ship.

When the term flying saucer was coined, it certainly described the appearance of many UFO sightings, but unfortunately, it eclipsed another important type of craft about which there are not only controversial theories but controversial photographs as well. For approximately each twenty authenticated flying saucer sightings, there is one report of a large, cigar-shaped craft which is, in theory, the mother ship from which the smaller but manned flying saucers operate.

One of the very early cigar craft sightings was made in 1897 by Alexander Hamilton, a farmer from Le Roy, Kan., who stepped to his door one April afternoon to witness an air ship descending upon his cow lot some 600 feet from the house. In a sworn and notarized statement, farmer Hamilton said his UFO "consisted of a great, cigar-shaped portion, possibly three hundred feet long." He also said the craft was manned by "six of the strangest beings I ever saw."

Possibly Hamilton was describing a dirigible, but dirigibles are not noted for giving off a dark reddish glow, nor were the early models likely to have as a power source "a giant turbine wheel, about thirty feet in diameter." For those who argue that Hamilton saw a dirigible, it is just as easy to rebut with the claim that a 300-foot craft of any kind was an anachronism for 1897.

Returning to more modern days, the UFO referred to in the Chiles–Whitted incident of 1948 was described as cigar shaped, about 100 feet long, and about twice the diameter of a B-29 Superfortress bomber.

On April 19, 1952, the then United Press reported that hundreds of Texans claimed to have seen UFOs in the sky over Dallas, Fort Worth, Austin, and Clarendon. Most of the UFOs were described as saucers, but there were reports of a banana-shaped object as well, adding further fuel to the theory that the large, tubular UFOs might be saucer carriers. A Fort Worth Air Force veteran who had logged 3600 hours of flying time produced pictures he'd taken of the bananalike objects.

A blue-green, cigar-shaped object made appearances in the skies over Washington, Oregon, and Idaho on August 11, 1950. Seen by more than one hundred persons, the object reportedly moved quite rapidly on a horizontal course, shone so brightly that it showed a noticeable disc, and, supposedly, broke into three pieces before disappearing.

Donald H. Menzel tries to write this sighting off as a part of the Perseid shower, an annual astronomical display of shooting stars and meteorites which takes place on or about August 11. But Menzel's theories have been demonstrated to have some holes in them, and official records still show this particular sighting to be unclassified. The supposed breaking up of this craft into three pieces could be taken as the launching of three smaller craft.

George Adamski, an amateur astronomer and restaurant worker who lives near the Mount Palomar Observatory in San Diego County, Calif., had an extremely good run of luck so far as the mother craft are concerned. Adamski's interest in UFOs and his strange experiences with them will be discussed later. Working through his 6-inch telescope, Adamski had produced hundreds of UFO photographs, mostly of the saucer variety. On March 5, 1951, Adamski used his telescope to make an amazing series of four photos. In the first photo, we see a huge, shadowy object which greatly resembles a blunt cigar. Above this is a saucer-shaped glow. With each successive photo, he caught the cigar-shaped craft with additional saucerlike forms, and in his fourth exposure, he has six disc-shaped forms, all apparently launched from the cigar craft.

On May 1, 1952, Adamski was again successful in photographing a cigar-shaped UFO which he said hovered over a mountain peak some 30 miles away from him. No saucers are visible in this shot, but the cigar is much more detailed.

Adamski swears the photos are unretouched, that they were developed and printed for him by another individual whom he trusted, and that any monies he may have taken in from the sale of these photos or from subsequent lectures were still not sufficient to cover his own expenses in his attempts to make photographs of UFOs and contacts with the beings in them.

On the night of November 2, 1957, four Texas police officers saw a huge glowing object which seemed to hover over the highway near Levelland, just in front of their car. The object was cigar shaped, about 200 feet long, and glowing a bluish-green color. After hovering just above the highway—one of the officers said it actually rested on the road—the cigar craft turned bright red, rose swiftly into the air, and moved off in the direction of the White Sands Proving Ground in New Mexico.

The Mount Shasta region in Tehama County, northern California, had a series of UFO incidents in 1960 which, if nothing else, added new respect for stories of mysterious lights in the area, stories which continue to proliferate. Nearly every night during the week of August 12 to 20, dozens of reports flocked in, claiming sightings of UFOs with red and white lights, yellow-colored saucers, and cigar-shaped objects with long, fiery exhausts.

Some attempts were made to write these sightings off as freaks of weather, but many viewers reported behavior patterns that simply do not coincide with any known atmospheric phenomena, and the official decision was to keep these Tehama County sightings on the books as presently unsolved. Here, again, the behavior seems to indicate the strong possibility that the cigar-shaped objects might have been discharging or taking on smaller, saucer-shaped craft.

In 1962 and 1964, cigar-shaped objects were reported over

Manhattan Beach, Calif., and Port Redding, N.J., respectively, with the identical results that there were scores of saucer sightings as far as 500 miles away in each instance.

Back in northern California again, a series of incidents in small towns near San Francisco brought in eyewitness reports, some from policemen, of dirigible or cigar-shaped objects, hovering in the sky and glowing red. These reports, however, gave the estimated size of the objects as about fifteen feet in length, opening the possibility for speculation that perhaps the larger cigars are mother ships for the bigger saucers, which we'll examine in a moment, while the smaller cigar may be one type of mother ship for the foo discs.

At any rate, these last two northern California descriptions of cigars, which came in 1964 and 1965 and were well corroborated, seem to be among the smallest size descriptions of the tubular craft. The modern record for sighting a large cigar craft would seem to belong to a Minnesota astronomer who, while traveling to California by train, looked out his window one evening in 1955 and made quite a discovery. He saw a cigar estimated at 800 feet long, moving through the Nevada night. The cigar craft he saw was soon joined by a large saucer, yet another case auguring for the mother ship theory.

As a general category, the flying saucer seems to have the most variations in size and shape, ranging from the flat disc to an oval, a bell, an ice cream cone, and even a pyramid.

An object which looked like a 30-foot ice cream cone was seen by five residents of San Leandro, Calif., an Oakland suburb, on February 9, 1950. The object also flew over the nearby Alameda Naval Air Station at a height of approximately 5,000 feet.

Slightly more than a month later, a small oil town in New

Mexico, a scant 100 miles from the Los Alamos atomic installation, was witness to a spectacular display of UFOs in which several varieties were spotted. On March 18, 1950, nearly half the residents of Farmington, N.M.—including private pilots and the entire staff of the newspaper—saw objects in the sky which they described as saucer and cone shaped, of varying sizes. Many had colored blinking lights. Estimates of the number of craft in this huge armada ran from a conservative "several" to as high as five hundred. Estimates of the speed of these saucers ran to a carefully conservative 1000 miles an hour. Sizes were reported in excess of the size of a B-29 bomber. One witness to the mass sighting said that the saucers he saw, viewed from the ground, appeared to be the size of a dinner plate. "They flew sideways, on edge, and at every conceivable angle. This is what made it easy to determine they were saucer shaped."

Reports of UFO sightings by veteran commercial or military pilots, aloft in their own planes, are no longer exceptional. But two closely spaced 1952 "in air" sightings certainly tend to emphasize the amazing maneuverability potential of UFOs.

In March of 1952, two pilots operating a commercial C-54 cargo plane from Chicago to Kansas City saw a silvery disc closing fast. The object seemed to retain its relative position to the plane for five or six minutes before the pilot of the C-54 decided to do some checking. He made a gradual turn toward the UFO and appeared to be narrowing the gap between them, but then the UFO began to veer off to the left.

Pilot and copilot both decided the object was a balloon and resumed their heading to Kansas City. Yet, minutes later, the UFO was still on their left. Now the pilot began making calculations. If the UFO were a balloon, they should be leaving it behind them. As a test, he made a 45-degree turn. The balloon appeared to lose ground, but not that much ground. Suddenly, it put on speed so as to make a turn outside the direction the C-54 was now taking. The C-54 was kept in a turn position until it had described a complete 360-degree maneuver. The UFO followed, keeping itself outside the C-54's turn at all times. Even though the C-54 is not a particularly fast aircraft nor noted for great feats of maneuverability, both the pilot and copilot were able to reason, and quite correctly, that their UFO not only could not be a balloon, it must be a comparatively fast vehicle, one of great agility.

Another UFO incident, which could be included with the classic sightings because of its popularity among researchers, is valuable here for at least three important reasons: the witnesses were highly competent, their descriptions were abundant and detailed, and we are given another indication of the versatile saucers. The Chesapeake Bay or Nash–Fortenberry incident took place after sunset on the night of June 14, aboard a Pan-American DC-4 flight en route from New York to Miami. At the controls were first officer William Nash, a pilot with thousands of hours of air time to his credit, and second officer William Fortenberry.

Cruising over the Chesapeake Bay at 8,000 feet, the DC-4 was just north of Norfolk, Virginia. Nash was pointing out cities and landmarks of the route to Fortenberry, who was new to this locale. At 8:12 P.M. a red glow appeared in the west, moving on a horizontal plane about 1 mile below the DC-4 and traveling at a tremendous rate of speed. As they watched through the cockpit windows, Nash and Fortenberry saw that the glow was, in reality, six lights of a red-orange hue. The six UFOs moved in a northeasterly direction until they were only about ½ mile from the DC-4.

Nash immediately guessed that the UFOs would pass under the window on Fortenberry's side. He unhitched his seat belt and moved to the copilot's side, but then an even stranger event took place. Nash and Fortenberry had already noted that the UFOs were quite sharply defined as narrow discs which were arranged in an echelon or step formation. The leader of this staggered formation was in the lowest position, number two UFO was slightly above him, number three UFO staggered farther above number two, etc.

Before Nash could move to Fortenberry's window and locate the UFOs, they had abruptly flipped on edge and reversed their direction. As Fortenberry described it, the amazing reversal of direction involved the saucers flipping up on their edge, like coins. While on edge, and with no further turn or maneuvering, they were able to reverse their direction.

By the time Nash gained his place on Fortenberry's side of the cabin, he was able to see the discs as they flipped back into a flat position. But this wasn't all. The discs, now proceeding in reverse order—with the former leader of the formation being the highest and last saucer in this new heading—suddenly changed directions again. They described an amazing turn of 270 degrees and streaked off toward the west. Two more saucers seemed to appear from directly under the DC-4; they joined the streaking formation as numbers seven and eight, then the entire formation disappeared. Moments later, they all reappeared, angling rapidly for an altitude well above the DC-4. Then they disappeared for the final time.

The best way to imagine the most incredible part of this UFO movement is to visualize a huge V. As the six saucers streak down one leg of the V, imagine them suddenly turning on edge just as they approach the apex, completely reversing their direction, flipping back to a flat position, then taking off along the final leg of the V.

Other flying saucer incidents seem to corroborate the variety of shapes and sizes.

In late 1961, a man and wife, returning from a Canadian vacation were buzzed by a large saucer which later, according to their reports, landed, took them aboard, and subjected them to intensive physical examinations. The saucer could have been as large around as 60 feet and was probably at least 15 feet high. The stories of both husband and wife were checked—individually first, then jointly and under hypnosis—by a prominent Boston psychiatrist, who is reasonably convinced of the accuracy and sincerity of their stories, even if he is more cautious about expressing his own beliefs in UFOs.

Two men who live near Ely, Nev., saw a pyramid-shaped object with a point that tapered down to a 2-foot pedestal. The object spun rapidly and bore an emblem or insignia, which they had difficulty making out because of the spinning movement of the entire object. This took place on July 1, 1964. The man who saw the emblem said it was definitely red in color, making an interesting comparison with another 1964 sighting near Socorro, N.M.

In this sighting, a Socorro police officer, Lonnie Zamora, was close enough to a UFO to see a symbol on the side. The symbol consisted of a horizontal bar. Directly over this bar was an arrow. Covering both the bar and arrow was a single curved line, very reminiscent of the plastic dome used to cover donuts in restaurants.

Two 1965 UFO incidents left traces of physical disturbances and an additional sighting resulted in another set of amazing photographs.

The physical disturbances were automobile failure and the traces of a huge burned-out area. The automobile failure case, one of scores on record, took place on the night of January 25, near Williamsburg, Va., when a reliable witness reported his automobile would not work after a huge, circular machine dropped down out of the sky and hovered near him. The witness could not get his car engine to turn over. Immediately after the huge disc lifted off and disappeared, the driver was able to operate his automobile again.

Two months later, a professional dog trainer was in the Florida Everglades when he saw mysterious, glowing lights. Investigating, he saw a huge disc resting on the dense grass. With an estimated height of 25 feet, the disc was described as being anywhere from 75 to 100 feet in diameter, and containing four tiers of lighted windows. The dog trainer approached the object and suddenly found himself lying flat on his back, stunned. When he regained his wits, he saw that the huge disc had left. In its wake was a scorched area in the grass, a perfect circle of 72 feet in diameter. In addition, trees and shrubs adjacent to the huge circle were also singed.

The photographs came from a sighting on August 3, 1965, when a Los Angeles County employee stopped his truck along a country road near Santa Ana to take shots of a UFO greatly resembling a flat-brimmed straw hat. Because he had two cameras, this man was able to get three remarkable shots, all showing the UFO at different attitudes. Although they are not closeups, the photos give a clear indication of the shape and some amount of detail including, in one photo, evidences of ground disturbance, as if from an exhaust or jet stream, swirling up a rise of dust.

These photos compare favorably with a series taken in 1952 by George Adamski, whom we've already met in connection with the cigar craft. He insists that his photos of bell-shaped craft and his claims to have boarded and flown in them, as well as talking to the operators, prove that they are Venusian in origin. Adamski is not the only person, by the way, to make all these claims.

His photos of the bell-shaped craft were given rather perfunctory treatment by Donald Menzel, who said they were nothing more than a chicken brooder, a heating and incubating device used to hatch baby chicks. Adamski's photographs show a bell-shaped object with portholes and a distinctive landing gear arrangement consisting of three triangularly placed giant ball bearings. A coil is partially visible as it circumnavigates the structure just above the portholes. At the top of the saucer is a large loop, which has been described as a directional antenna that picks up power from magnetic force lines and as a convenient hook by which the craft is stored in the cigar-shaped mother ship.

We'll have more to say about Menzel and Adamski in later chapters. For the moment, let it suffice that Adamski swears his photos are genuine, the Venusian bell craft is quite real, and that he has ridden in them. Let it also suffice that Menzel has had Adamski's photo reduced to a schematic drawing, reduced the underside of a chicken brooder to a schematic drawing, reproduced the two on the same page and let the similarity speak loudly for itself.

This is only one of the interesting and heated battles raging over what is real, what is hoax, and what is illusion in the long, amazing history of the UFO.

CHAPTER FOUR

Emissaries from the Past

For almost every modern event of importance, such as the assassination of a president, the founding of a new country, the entering into of an alliance, the development of a new cure, the discovery of a new element, or the witnessing of a new phenomenon, there may be found an ancient reference or prediction.

Two of the most popular source books for such ancient predictions are the Bible and the oracles of Nostradamus. More esoteric works such as the Tibetan *Book of the Dead* and the Hindu scriptures may be consulted with great success. The only seeming barriers to making such after-the-fact associations would be lack of sufficient books and lack of sufficient imagination.

UFOs are no exception to this rule, and as thinly documented and tenuous as some modern reports are, some of the ancient mystical, religious, and occult books are certainly plentiful in their suggestions that UFOs—although not by that name—visited the earth, were manned by some form of human or near-human beings, and that their purposes and destinies were intimately linked with our forebears.

Until we are able to establish more definitive contacts with the beings who pilot UFOs and corroborate their exact intentions and the precise history of their visits to earth, drawing inferences about such activities before the early 1900's falls more into the category of a hobby than anything else. An interesting hobby, no question about it. Because it is just as possible that some of the more unlikely interpretations will prove out to be true as it is likely that the more thoroughly witnessed or seemingly scientific observations will prove out.

Many of the civilian UFO study groups who now claim some form of contact with the beings who use UFOs are engaged in this kind of saucer lore, attempting to extract from their discussions and studies a sort of universal, modern, and pragmatic means of life. To pass off their philosophies as mere religious study is to do them disservice. And even though Air Force and more scientifically oriented UFO study groups might write off these civilian groups as part of the immense lunatic fringe often associated with UFOs, the newly interested UFO fan owes himself a serious look at all the aspects.

For a brief look at some of these out-of-the-ordinary saucer theories, Biblical interpretation presents an excellent focus.

Discussing the ascension of Christ into the sky, author Morris K. Jessup suggests that some form of levitation or teleportation was involved and says the least disturbing solution to this matter lies in the possibility of the presence of a UFO to lift Him into the clouds. The irony here is that such a possibility is often the *most* disturbing solution to the newcomer who is earnestly investigating some of the existing UFO theories, and there have been cases where first- or second-time visitors to saucer study groups have found themselves grossly offended or shattered with amazement that adults could seriously be considering the prophets as extraterrestrials, much less intimating that Christ, Himself, could be considered as a former inhabitant of another planet.

34

Yet in recent years, with the scientific community showing more inclination to believe that other planets in other galaxies might support intelligent life, church spokesmen are becoming enthusiastic and vocal on the subject. Roman Catholic prelates are already on record as believing that the discovery of intelligent human or humanlike life on other planets will in no way weaken the tenets and faiths of the Church.

Morris Jessup throws an intriguing barb into this subject by discussing the story of the ascent into heaven of Elijah, the prophet. Our attention is called to II Kings, chapter 2, verse 11: "And it came to pass, as they still went on, and talked, that behold, there appeared a chariot of fire, and horses of fire, and parted them Elijah and Elisha both asunder; and Elijah went up by a whirlwind into Heaven."

Jessup begins zeroing in on his extensive theories by quoting the belief of a Biblical scholar that the Aramic words for whirlwind, *ruach cearah* should properly be translated as power blast. Taking the same verse from II Kings, Jessup brings his own modern, UFO-oriented translation: "As they walked and talked there suddenly appeared a bright UFO, emitting electric sparks and blasts, and it parted them; Elijah was snatched up into the sky with a blast of power."

Too many descriptions of fiery chariots, wheel-like discs, and glows in the sky appear in the Bible for Jessup and similar devotees to ignore the similarity to descriptions of the sightings already discussed so far. In direct contrast to many modern Biblical interpretations, Jessup advocates assuming that the Bible means literally and physically what it says. Starting with a brief quote from the Gospel according to St. Luke at 21:25, the suggestion that Biblical events and past UFO events are linked takes on a strong significance with such quotes as "And there shall be signs in the Sun, and in the Moon, and in the stars . . ."

Jessup's two important studies, *The Case for the UFO* and *UFO and the Bible* merit study for a fascinating background to the enigma unidentified objects in the skies have presented to man through the ages. And it is no accident that some UFO study groups have become convinced that the UFO is one of the great common denominators of all time, linking religious, metaphysical, and mystical theories with reality.

Following Jessup's enjoinder to take the passages from the Bible literally, let's look briefly at a few other choice quotations from the King James version.

Ezekiel 1:4–5 "As I looked and behold, a whirlwind came out of the north, a great cloud, and a fire unfolding itself, and a brightness was about it, and out of the midst, thereof, as the color of amber, out of the midst of the midst of the fire. Also out of the midst, thereof, came the likeness of four living creatures. And this was their appearance; they had the likeness of a man."

Ezekiel 1:28 and 2:1 "This was the appearance of the likeness of the glory of the Lord. And when I saw it, I fell upon my face, and I heard a voice of one that spake. And he said unto me, Son of Man, stand upon thy feet, and I will speak unto thee."

Zechariah 5:1–2 "Again I lifted my eyes and saw, and behold, a flying roll. The length thereof is twenty cubits and the breadth thereof ten cubits."

To continue with the heavenly implications while changing from the Christian beliefs to Hindu proposes no conflict along these lines. Vishnu, one of the three great Hindu deities, was of heavenly origin. The *Ramayana* is a scripture dealing with Rama, one of Vishnu's incarnations. It is filled with accounts of large aircraft, some powered by forces beyond human ken. Here are some examples that tend to lend themselves well toward modern UFO descriptions:

"When morning dawned, Rama, taking the celestial car . . . stood ready to depart. Self-propelled was that car . . . It was large and finely painted. It had two stories and many chambers with windows . . . It gave forth a melodious sound as it coursed along its airy way."

Another quote reads: "The . . . car that resembles the sun . . . was brought by the powerful Ravan; that aerial and excellent car, going everywhere at will, is ready for thee. That car, resembling a bright cloud in the sky . . ."

The three-thousand-year-old epic poem *Mahabharata,* written in Sanskrit, has its references too. "A blazing missile . . . of the radiance of smokeless fire was discharged . . ." This missile spins, radiates light, is operated by a circular reflecting device, and leaves a wake of great, scorching heat.

Other Sanskrit descriptions are plentiful and, interestingly enough, these writings are divided into two important groups, *daiva;* which was an admitted myth, and *manusa;* which was offered as the strictest of fact. One important *manusa* is the *Samarangana Sutradhara* which discusses flying disclike objects which could ascend on a vertical line, extend their operations over thousands of miles, halt, hover, and move with great agility.

Ancient Tibetan books discuss flying objects that give off a glow, and were used by persons of a certain religious degree. In other ancient manuscripts in addition to the ones mentioned, there are constant references to travel between planets.

Returning to more modern times, we might pause for a

slight digression in the year 1290. The place, Byland Abbey in Yorkshire, England. According to an old manuscript turned up in 1953, there were a few contretemps in the abbey. Just as Henry, the Abbott, was about to say grace over some roasted sheep which commemorated the feast of Saints Simon and Jude, one of the brothers rushed inside to announce that "there was a great portent outside." When the brothers dashed outside, "a large round silver thing like a disc flew slowly over them and excited the greatest terror."

About two hundred years later, a silvery, disc-shaped object played merry hell over a church in Ireland during a morning mass. The disc skimmed the area several times and, with its trailing exhaust, managed to dislodge a bell from its mooring, singe a few cows, and frighten the parish. No record of the subsequent sermon exists, but it may be safe to assume that the good father used the opportunity to get in a few choice words about the possibilities of fire and brimstone.

An Italian monastery reports seeing glowing discs in the sky in the late 1500's. In Scotland, a few years later, a long, tubular object appeared, was seen by many inhabitants of a small community, hovered for several minutes, then disappeared.

In Fluelen, Switzerland, in 1619, an enormous, long, fiery object was seen flying alongside a lake.

1644 was the date of a sighting at sea. The log of a Spanish merchant vessel is reported to contain references to a formation of bright, glowing objects which blazed across the sky, then seemed to jump about wildly, resume formation, then streak up for higher altitudes.

Nearly a century later, Florence, Italy, had reports of strange globes of light in the sky which appeared on December 9, 1731.

The year of 1755 was a traumatic one for Lisbon, Portugal. The day and night of October 15 was the finale of a series of sightings in which large globes appeared to cavort in the sky.

Two years later, a British astronomer said he saw wildly maneuvering objects changing colors as they sped through the sky, then moved off at an impossible angle.

Two Swiss astronomers saw an enormous spindle-shaped object which was surrounded by a glowing outer ring. The sighting was made on August 9, 1762. One of the astronomers made his reported sighting from Basel, the other from Sole.

A third memorable sighting of UFOs by an astronomer came in the eighteenth century when Charles Messier, a noted Frenchman, reported his spotting of several large, round discs in the sky.

As easy as it has been for modern skeptics to write off the glowing objects, spinning saucers, and large, tubular phenomena of recent years as freaks of the atmosphere, shooting stars, cloud formations, and actual planets, any amount of faith put in these dated sightings seems to be truly in jeopardy. Look at all the possibilities for rebuttal. What did the ancients know of astronomy? How many of the ancients were sophisticated? How many had a true scientific approach to the problem?

The *idée fixe* of the UFO skeptics is that the ancient and modern sightings are both natural phenomena, nothing else. Seen strictly as a recurrent ancient theme, these earlier sightings might not tend to hold water, even if some of them include the presence of strange-looking people as well as strange-looking craft. When we begin to consider some of the still old but much more recent sightings of the nineteenth century, we still have the hue and cry of optical illusion and hallucination, both from critics contemporary to the age and from modern critics. And by the time we bring our survey up into the twentieth century and well along into the 1960's, this hue and cry begins to seem more dated, more paranoid, and more unscientific than the most imaginative interpretations given to UFOs.

Although the descriptions of alleged UFO sightings through the years remain fairly constant in description, at least some of the behavior and motives attributed to them seems to undergo a pragmatic change. But it may be successfully argued that the anti-UFO theories of such stalwarts as Dr. Donald Menzel have changed very little over the years and are more in the tradition of resisting change than the theories of such outspoken UFO fans as Mrs. Coral Lorenzen, the director of the Aerial Phenomena Research Organization (APRO).

Assuming that even a small percentage of the nineteenth century UFO sightings are valid, there are a few distinct points which should be borne in mind before any of the details are given.

The beginning of the nineteenth century marked the flowering of another phenomenon that had been budding for long years, and by the time the noted German astronomer Fritsch saw UFOs in 1802, the Industrial Revolution was already under a full head of steam, its momentum clearly defined, its influence on the world of shattering importance. Scientific discoveries, advancements in industry, and a spirit of investigation started in England, spread to the new world, flared up with an especial brilliance in America, and became the grandparent, if not the actual parent, of the current age of development.

If we accept one of the many UFO theories—the one which says these craft from other worlds are watching us and our development to determine the appropriate moment for a full-scale contact—it is likely that the UFO intelligences certainly would have had a great interest in the doings of nineteenth century earth. As we look at some of the following nineteenth century sightings, let's try to keep in mind how exciting these times were: tremendous social reforms; intensive interest in astronomy, in the refinement of machinery; Darwin and his theory of evolution; the development of gadgetry; intensive psychical research, reaching new heights and suggesting strongly that man was interested in making the same gigantic discoveries within himself that he had been making in the physical world.

These were the days of flashing lights in the sky at Tottenham, Middlesex, England. In 1816, more sightings in the sky over Lisbon. And that very same year, huge, crescent-shaped aircraft were seen crossing the horizon in Edinburgh, Scotland.

At the very beginning of 1818, an Ipswich astronomer made the remarkable sighting of a strange object which hovered near the sun for three and a half hours.

Previews of the present-day formations of UFOs and their great agility come in 1820. On three separate occasions—February 12, April 27, and September 7—formations of flying objects cross Emburn in the southeast of France. They streak through the skies, make sudden, 90-degree turns, then fly swiftly away.

In 1822, an astronomer sees a recurrence of an already commonplace phenomenon: two unknown objects are sighted as they move past the sun's disc.

A year later, an English astronomer sees an extraordinary shining object near Venus.

Then, in 1826, in Saarbrucken, France, a grey torpedo is seen as it moves rapidly toward the earth. But no crashes of any sort are reported.

Across the continent in Ohio, a brilliant, hook-shaped object is seen hovering in the sky. The time, 1833. In November of the same year, a large luminous aircraft puzzles and baffles onlookers at Niagara Falls, N.Y.

In the intervening years, a few more astronomers make reports of strange movements and odd formations. Then, in 1836, a huge craft is seen hovering over the city of Cherbourg, France. It is shaped very much like a donut and is observed to be spinning about its own axis from time to time.

More sightings take place, in India, Chile, Argentina, and on ships at sea. Some of the UFOs seem to be spouting luminous orange tails. Critics of these reports cite astronomical phenomena as solutions. Astronomers join the battle and insist their sightings were not comets, shooting stars, or any heavenly displays known to man.

As 1845 is ushered in, there are political changes in England. The laborers are asking for greater parliamentary reforms. A murderous blight hits the Irish potato crop, ruining the staple product of that country and leaving thousands to starve. In that same year, stationary orange objects are seen hovering over London.

An Italian astronomer sees a fleet of shining discs moving from west to east over the city of Naples. Some of these objects are star-shaped and have shiny, luminous tails.

Less than a month later, a ship at sea notices three huge discs, apparently rising from the water. They remain visible for nearly ten minutes and are reported to be of fantastic proportions and connected by bright, glowing streamers. These huge craft are seen by observers as far away as 900 miles. The descriptions generally agree.

A month later, another sighting is made in Florence, Italy. A huge, fiery disc scuds overhead, traveling leisurely at first, then putting on an intense burst of speed as it disappears.

Perhaps they are emissaries from other worlds, having a look. Now and then, they leave behind them something more tangible than a memory of a mysterious vision. In 1846, a large, shiny disc appeared over Lowell, Mass., and dropped a lump of "most fetid-smelling jelly which was found to weigh 442 pounds, and was 4 feet in diameter." Other reports of similar jellylike substances come in and the opinions and theories fly, but no one knows what the substance is.

Five months later, back in England, several Londoners spotted a blazing spherical craft as it rose vertically into the clouds. A year later, Inverness, Scotland, experiences two large, bright objects which hover and then dart about the sky at great speeds.

Then, in 1849, an astronomer in Switzerland looks on as witness to thousands of luminous objects moving across a clear sky.

Sightings continue. Fiery balls and luminous discs compete for attention. Even at this time, the apparent variety of shapes is manifest.

In 1852, with Venus at the point of closest approach to Earth a strange luminous disc is seen near that planet.

A cigar-shaped object, a large round ball and a small disc are seen near the planet Mercury in 1853. That same year, a flying machine is reported. It is still some time before the Wright Brothers will have made their short but significant heavier than air flight at Kitty Hawk, N.C.

Once again, with Venus close to earth, a glowing red disc is seen on August 11, 1855. The disc is described as having wheel-like spokes. Rays project from it and it is visible for ninety minutes.

A flying torpedo puts in an appearance over France in 1856, and another long, cigar-shaped craft is noted over the south of England in 1864. His craft is luminous and tapered at both ends, a description that fits the George Adamski cigar craft photograph of nearly a hundred years later.

On June 8, 1868, the position of Venus is close to earth. Observers at the Radcliffe Observatory, Oxford, see a blazing red spot on that normally misty planet. A luminous object is seen in the sky. It halts, changes its course heading to west, to south, then north. All in all, it has been in view for nearly four minutes.

The *Lady of the Lake* is at sea when the captain and crew spot a frightening sight skimming along just under the clouds. The rear half of this circular object is surrounded by a fuzz which is divided into four sections. A long, curved tail extends from the center of the object. It remains visible for some time and then is obscured by clouds. The year, 1870.

With Venus close to the earth again, a huge red disc is seen hovering over Marseilles, France, on August 1, 1871. The time is 10:43 P.M. The unusually large disc remains hovering for nine minutes, moves north, hovers again, then moves east. It is after 11:00 P.M. when the object finally disappears from sight.

Less than a month later, a French astronomer reports a group of formations in the sky. Some of the UFOs are saucer shaped, others are triangular, round, and multisided. One of the discs appears to fall, as though it had gone completely out of control. An explosion is seen, but no traces are discovered.

The Mexicans who observe the strange appearance over the

sky of Oaxaca do not know what to make of the huge craft. The estimated size is 400 feet. The UFO is trumpet shaped. It appears to hover in the sky for a full six minutes. The date is July 6, 1874.

The late 1870's are filled with reports of glowing objects and then, in October of 1877, an incident takes place which, in retrospect, looks very much as if UFOs are engaged in a program of observation. Eight luminous bodies, flying in a perfect formation, appear over the Wales coast, skimming up and back as though they are searching for something. They appear night after night, moving along the coast, following the contours of the land. Perhaps they were charting the coast or observing the tides.

Into the 1880's and before the first year of that decade is finished, a long, cigar-shaped craft is seen over France. A smaller disc is later seen leaving the cigar.

Two years later, the famed Greenwich Observatory sees a remarkable torpedo, moving from 40 miles to 200 miles in height. "Nothing could be more unlike a meteor," observers say, "and too fast for a cloud." The torpedo definitely appears to be a solid body. This sighting is also apparent to observers in Belgium and Holland.

And then there is the "comet" of August 29, 1883. Or is it a comet? It is seen alternately on one side of the Atlantic and then the other, with a beam like a searchlight probing out from the nucleus. Some comet.

We have a bit more than sixty years to go before the Kenneth Arnold sighting in 1947. Still, we may be more than generous; we may arbitrarily discard half the previous sightings as a combination of the worst kind of hallucination and astronomical phenomena. Still, there is a convincing body of sightings remaining.

But they are only the beginning.

CHAPTER FIVE

Closer to the Present—Closer to the Truth?

It is not very difficult to look back at the past and wonder what effects, if any, the strange and mysterious sightings in the skies had on the people of the nineteenth century. Even with the sophistication of satellites, lunar probes, and those extraordinary photos beamed back to earth from the moon safely under our belts, we are by no means blasé in our reactions to contemporary UFO sightings.

Certainly Norman Muscarello was far from blasé when he stumbled into the police station at Exeter, N.H., early on the morning of September 3, 1965, to announce the awesome thing he had seen. Muscarello's "thing" came out of the air, directly toward him, noiselessly. It was as big as a house and perhaps 90 feet in diameter. It seemed to float before him and appeared for a time that it was actually going to hit him. His fear quickly became the fear of a small town, and of thousands of people over a thousand miles away in Michigan. His fear could easily have been the fear of the people living in the tail end of the nineteenth century.

In March, 1893, a luminous construction is seen in the skies over France. Two months later, an English ship, the *H.M.S. Caroline*, en route between Shanghai and Japan, was witness to a squadron of discs for a period of two hours. Seen through a telescope, these discs were red in color and emitted brown smoke trails.

Back in England, a bright disc, larger than the planet Venus (as seen from earth) is seen rising over a clump of trees and traveling toward the east. Three days later, it is seen in Yorkshire, moving at a slow pace, as if looking for something or watching something or, perhaps, charting something. Both sighting sources agree that the object could not be the planet Venus since it was considerably brighter than that body. These sightings take place in 1895.

Nearly a year later, a long black cigar is observed as it crosses the moon's disc. This is also the year when saucerlike discs are observed in fiery formation over San Rafael and San Francisco, Calif. And in the following year, West Coast UFO reports take a sharp increase.

Moving over to Omaha, Neb., we find the report of a mysterious craft that put in its third appearance on the night of March 29, 1897. A contemporary newspaper report said the airship was "in the shape of a big bright light, too big for a balloon." It glowed steadily and sailed directly over Omaha, finally disappearing behind houses and bluffs to the northwest. The newspaper report said the sighting was made by a number of reputable citizens and was seen by people in all parts of the city.

The very next day, a bizarre report involving this ship or one like it came from Sioux City, Iowa. A farmer reportedly was dragged several yards by a rope with a hook, both of which dangled from this aircraft. The newspaper account said the farmer's reputation for truth had always been high.

Not discounting the possibilities of some April Fool's Day hijinks, a Decatur, Mich., account of that day in 1897 told of an airship that passed over the village the previous night, emitting a strange bright light and a huge black object from which human voices were heard.

What did these voices say? Were they distinguishable as speaking English or any recognizable language? The answer must be an emphatic toss of the head. For all the dated reports of people hearing voices in connection with their UFO sightings, the overwhelming favorite selection of the language they heard being spoken was Chinese. But the probability of these people being able to recognize Chinese or any similar-sounding language remains problematical.

The Chicago *Tribune* made reports of another sighting at Omaha. On April 6, the *Tribune* said, several hundred people insisted they saw an airship, a steel body estimated at 12 to 15 feet in length. Whatever it was, this craft appeared to have mobility. On April 9, the *Tribune* carried another story: the craft was seen by hundreds of persons "whose honesty and truthfulness are beyond dispute." This incident was 128 miles from Chicago at Mt. Carroll, Ill. Moving along in the general vicinity, the craft moved to Wausau, Wisconsin, where it was seen by at least a hundred persons who said an egg shape and bright lights could be discerned. This was also reported on April 9.

UFOs seemed firmly entrenched in midwestern America. A day later, some form of flying object put in an appearance at Galesburg, Ill., where it remained in sight for fifteen minutes, giving off an intense white light. This was April 10, the same day a sighting was made by a policeman and several other persons in Elgin, Ill. Their description, "It was in outline, like a ship, showing a red, blue, and large white light." The ubiquitous craft, or something like it, put in an appearance over Eldora, Iowa and also on the 10th, two thousand Iowans from Newton were on the streets at eight in the evening, watching a flying craft that appeared to drop a parachute with a light attached to it. We have no record if the parachute was ever recovered or what was attached to it, but the strong suggestion that the ship which dropped this parachute was not alone in the area came as a result of a report from Ottumwa, Iowa, the same night. A UFO appeared at Eldon, Iowa at 7:25, then Ottumwa at 7:40, and then at Albia at 8:10, where it remained in sight for ten minutes. This would seem to preclude its being the Eldora craft, which was seen at 8:00, where it allegedly remained for forty minutes.

Other reports came in from Kansas City and Chicago. Then, on the 16th of April, some UFO with green and red tail lights was seen at Benton, Texas. Other Texas towns reported cigar-shaped craft with enormous projections and two brilliant beams of light.

This very same day, according to the Topeka, Kan., *State Journal*, UFOs made a visit to Washington, D.C. Similar in description to the recent Chicago and Iowa sightings, this object was about 600 feet off the ground, sailing toward the Washington Monument, where it began to dip toward earth. Washington, D.C., residents were able to keep the UFO in sight for ten minutes before it disappeared behind the hills of Georgetown.

April of 1897 was a busy month in America for UFOs. On the 20th, the new target area was Sisterville, Va. The object seen was reported to be a huge "conical ship, 180 feet long, with fins on either side." As it sailed across the sky, it flashed bright red, green, and white lights. And already, some amount of skepticism is beginning to creep into the reports. In this instance, the question is raised that the UFO might be a balloon, but tacked onto the report is the terse notation that no balloons were known to be airborne at this time and in this area.

Then, on April 22, 1897, a peculiar sighting took place which had several elements in it that link it directly to the present times. Captain Jim Hooton, a railroad engineer, had gone to Texarkana, Tex., to bring back a special train. Faced with the prospect of an eight- to ten-hour layover, Hooton says he went to a nearby area for some hunting. He had good luck at his sport and was returning to the railroad station when he heard a noise that reminded him of the working of an air pump on a locomotive. Investigating, Hooton not only saw a strange object but had direct contact with the individuals in it. It is a tossup which was the more bizarre, Hooton's description of the strange craft he saw or his account of the individuals he saw.

His description of the craft is on record as a drawing. In it, we can see a large object like a silo set on end. One end is quite sharp, described by Hooton as being similar to the cowcatcher on a locomotive. Huge shields seem to spring out of the side and there are several wheel-like arrangements, also on the sides. An intricate rudder system and turbinelike apparatus complete the improbable picture. But both Capt. Hooton's drawing of the craft and the report of his conversation with one of the persons in it seem to have more relation to the recent Jack Lemmon motion picture, "The Great Race," than they do to the lore of UFOs.

Hooton says there was a medium-sized man aboard the craft. He appeared to be puttering near the back of the craft. He wore smoked glasses, noticed Hooton with some surprise, and said, "Good day, sir, good day." In his report, Hooton claims he asked this man if the craft were, indeed, *the* air ship, meaning the one that had been seen recently. The man wearing smoked glasses allegedly told Hooton it was. Apparently some of Hooton's amazement vanished. He claims to have remarked that the noise issuing from the craft sounded to him like a Westinghouse air brake. "Perhaps it does, my friend," came the rejoinder. "We are using condensed air and aeroplanes—but you will know more later on."

What Capt. Hooton knew more of later on was what such men of the 1950's as George Adamski, George Van Tassel, and Daniel Fry knew. In many quarters and in many newspaper and word-of-mouth retellings of the event, the good engineer found scorn, disbelief, and the conviction that he had lost his mind. He became, on that day, probably the first American to claim a contact at close range with a UFO and with the people in it. To complete his story, Hooton says that a voice called out, "All ready, sir!" and then the flying party all disappeared below. Moments later, the strange craft was aloft, and in comparatively short time later, it was out of sight.

There are several elements to Capt. Hooton's story which, although they do not suggest he was lying, certainly try our credulity. A sharp, cowcatcher-like object at the front of the craft. A man wearing smoked glasses. Mysterious wheels that turn and flash. But wait. Does the Captain's story sound any less fantastic than the 1961 story of Barney and Betty Hill, who claim they were taken aboard a flying saucer and given a thorough medical examination by strange, extraterrestrial beings?

Seventy-five years of sightings have not made us any more sure of our ground. To be sure, there are immense possibilities that Capt. Hooton stumbled on a group of very dedicated and very earthly inventors, who were having a great run of success. But even if this were so and Capt. Hooton's smoked-glasses wearing leader was so successful with his "invention," doesn't it follow that some greater bid for nation-wide recognition would be made? An invention that had withstood so many tests would surely be worth making public.

From Capt. Hooton's description, his UFO was clearly not a balloon, dirigible, or other closely related craft. So, a few brief paragraphs on the state of the art of aircraft are warranted here. The time is 1897, and balloons have met with some degree of success, having reached the unprecedented heights of approximately 10,000 feet. The use of lighter-than-air gas had begun, replacing a phenomenon that, when seen from the ground, might possibly account for earlier UFO sightings. Early balloons relied on a fire basket, an actual fire compartment that was fed with fuel to insure a continuous supply of warm, rising air into the main balloon bag. Surely it may be argued that the sight of a blazing ball of fire, reflecting on a distant balloon bag, either during the day or night, might explain away many so-called UFOs.

At this point of development, the balloon was still at the mercy of the direction and speed of the air currents in which the craft floated. Some degree of maneuverability was possible, but not very much, and as late as 1900, prizes were being offered to the inventors of balloons who could, in effect, steer against prevailing air currents. One such prize, offered in 1900, was a hundred thousand francs. This challenge was not met successfully until October of the next year, when Santos-Dumont, a wealthy young Brazilian, succeeded, after six frustrating and often humorous attempts, to manipulate a motor-driven balloon over a rather short course in Paris. Santos-Dumont's experiments with sizes and shapes of motor-driven balloons eventually led to the development of blimps and dirigibles, but this development was slow.

During this time, considerable attention was given to another form of aircraft, the glider, and it became a matter of time before small 1-horsepower engines were tried out on these lighter-than-air craft, or modifications which had the power to balance a bit more surely on air currents. An early pioneer in this field was Professor Samuel P. Langley, the Secretary of the Smithsonian Institution at Washington, D.C. Langley actually made two trial flights in 1903, but they both resulted in wreckages and were marked by a nobleness of effort and, alas, a noble lack of control.

Wilbur and Orville Wright, at Kitty Hawk, N.C., made their epic flight on December 17, 1903. The most impressive of the runs made that day was over a distance of 852 feet in a little less than a minute. This was accomplished in an area chosen especially by the brothers for the constant and useful winds present. This was the day on which it had been demonstrated conclusively that man had a destiny in the sky, and if it appears that sport is being made of Santos-Dumont, Prof. Langley, or the Wright brothers, an apology is due. The emphasis on the rather limited successes is being made for another purpose.

Consider the year 1904, in Dayton, Ohio. Here, the Wright brothers, with the benefit of their Kitty Hawk experiences, produced a heavier-than-air craft that was able to stay aloft for five minutes and seventeen seconds, covering a distance of nearly 3 miles. They were also able to produce a circular flight. This was 1904.

These facts certainly make many of the pre-1900 sightings of UFOs sound more like unidentifiable objects and less like potential motor-driven aircraft. And it was still to be some time before a more stable, motor-powered airplane or dirigible would be produced that would seem to fit the descriptions of the UFOs of the 1800's.

Moving ahead into the 1900's, a survey of sighting reports shows at least one interesting incident per year. In 1907, Burlington, Vt., had a visit. A huge, dark torpedo hovered over the city, shooting tongues of fire and showers of sparks. The torpedo seemed to change color before it began to move off and, as it did so, a small disclike craft apparently detached itself. Shortly after, both UFOs disappeared.

Caerphilly, Wales, became the sight of the first twentieth century report of a UFO that had apparently landed. A Cardiff man claims he was walking through the mountains when he saw a long torpedo parked on the side of a road. Inside the torpedo were two "peculiar-looking" men, dressed in fur coats. They began chattering in a strange language, caused the craft to activate and move off rapidly but silently. The torpedo reportedly had no wings or any wing-like appendages. As if to confirm the fact that it had really been there, an indentation was found in the grass. This event took place in 1909.

The new year of 1910 had scarcely begun when the citizens of Chattanooga, Tenn., reported the presence of a mysterious white aircraft that came in from the north and appeared to be on a southeast heading. For the following two days, the UFO returned and was seen by thousands as it approached the city from a new direction each time.

An estimated million persons saw a monumental procession of UFOs as they crossed the skies over New York City on September 21, 1910. The disc-shaped objects flew over the city for nearly three hours, holding up traffic and commerce as people thronged the streets and craned their necks for a view.

By this time, the Wright brothers had had their early successes and were working diligently toward more. But their successes and the work of their contemporaries was hardly enough to match these 1900's sightings as a viable explanation for UFOs.

Within three years, Wales was again the scene of sightings, headed by accounts of a huge airship. A large tube with sweeping lights was also reported in the south of Wales.

The day before the official beginning of World War I, Herefordshire, England, was the scene of clusters of UFOs shaped like dumbbells. Subsequent events in that war revealed no flying object of any country involved which might have been mistaken for these strange objects.

In 1915, a cigar is seen hovering over Huntington, W.Va., and North Carolina reports that discs and other bright objects have been appearing overhead from 1920 to 1923.

A steamship 400 miles off the Virginia coast reports that on August 29, 1929, it witnessed a luminous body moving through the air at an estimated speed of 100 miles an hour. The fact that any heavier-than-air object is seen that far out is a phenomenon in itself.

Suddenly, we seem caught up. Seventeen years and ten months later, Kenneth Arnold spots the first of the modern classic UFO sightings, and with the assurance that there have been at least five hundred sightings in the intervening years, we have a pattern of UFO sightings that covers a span of at least three hundred years. This "record" can go even farther back to the dim reaches of time if we accept Morris Jessup's invitation to accept as literal some of the descriptions found in the Bible.

A modern scientist has suggested that we take all the accepted scientific theories and discoveries piled up by mankind since the beginning of recorded time and ending at 1950. If we place this tremendous weight of discovery on one side of an imaginary scale and place all the discoveries made in the fifteen years from 1950 to 1965, the balance will tip slightly in favor of contemporary times. With this log of new discovery at our disposal, we have an excellent opportunity of tripling the available amount of scientific knowledge. Still, we cannot be any surer of what the UFOs are, where they are from, and who controls them than we were in the nineteenth century. To be sure, there are excellent theories, supported by our greater awareness of the galaxy in which we live. But at the same time, we have come to understand how tremendously small our galaxy is in the overall scheme of things. And, if anything, we have greatly increased in our own minds the possible number of places from which UFOs could originate.

In 1920, the known universe was less than 200,000 light-years in diameter and was made up of our galaxy and two neighbors. But many theories and problems which were raised in the 1930's began to be resolved when, during the 1942 wartime blackouts, Walter Baade, an astronomer who had access to the Mount Wilson observatory in Los Angeles, made approaches to an amazing series of discoveries. The size of the known universe was more than doubled, solving earlier problems that had plagued scientists. Our galaxy was no longer accepted as being larger than all the others and, rather importantly, the age of the universe was estimated by Isaac Asimov as being at least five billion years old, an age which puts the universe more in line with the estimated age of the earth. Dr. Asimov, a copious writer and dedicated researcher, says that our own galaxy seems to be a part of a local cluster "that includes the Magellanic Clouds, the Andromeda galaxy, and three small 'satellite galaxies' near it, plus some other small galaxies for a total of seventeen members altogether. Of these, only two, our own galaxy and Andromeda, are giants, whereas the rest are dwarfs. One of them, IC 1613, may contain only sixty million stars."

Only sixty million stars. A piddling enough amount in proportion to other galaxies, but more important, where there are stars, there are planets and thus, from galaxy IC 1613 alone, if we arbitrarily assign each star two planets, we have one hundred twenty million potential places where intelligent life may be found within the confines of a dwarf galaxy.

With these discoveries and probabilities, we are in a position where we can set greater store by our observations and theories, we are in a position where we have greater and more accurate standards against which to measure UFO reports and, one would think, we would have much greater ammunition for proving, once and for all, that UFOs do or do not exist. At this stage of the game, we are certainly forced to conclude that they exist, and we are also forced to conclude that they mean us no harm at this time, nor have they meant us harm at any time in the past.

One UFO theory enjoying currency is well advanced by Donald E. Keyhoe, a retired Marine Corps major who has written copiously on UFOs and studied official reports avidly. He suggests as one possibility that earth has been under surveillance by a planet or planets with sun or suns going cold. To see if earth can support life, we are being examined as a potential place for colonization. And since modern astronomers estimate a two-to-five-billion-year life expectancy for earth, this might be a strong probability. Another UFO theory advanced is that earth is already a colony, that persons from other planets had been sent here and had grown away from the original life and culture.

One astounding theory that intelligent and well-advanced beings were once on this planet is advanced by Major Keyhoe in his report of the Piri Reis map incident. In the early part of the sixteenth century, Piri Reis, an admiral in the Turkish navy, completed work on a world chart. The year was 1513. As references for his chart, Piri Reis used a map that had once belonged to and had been used by Columbus. Reis also had access to Greek maps which dated to the time of Alexander the Great.

A portion of the Piri Reis chart, showing the coasts of South America, Africa, and sections of Antarctica was sent by a Turkish officer in 1953 to the Chief Engineer of the U.S. Navy Hydrographic Office for evaluation. This portion of the map was the only part known to be available. After giving the chart a detailed study, the Chief Engineer and his staff of advisors came to some remarkable conclusions:

Columbus had with him on his voyage to America a map which showed the coasts of Yucatan, Guatemala, South America to the Straits of Magellan, and an appreciable part of the coast of Antarctica. The original maps were at least five thousand years old, and some of the data went back even further into time. Part of the land areas shown on the maps in detail had been buried under ice for twenty centuries, possibly even longer.

Charts of such amazing accuracy could have been produced by chance or guess-work only at astronomically high odds. The far greater and more acceptable, if confusing, hypothesis was that the charts could have been produced only by highly competent survey teams and chart makers. A Navy authority on old maps, after working on the Piri Reis fragment and consulting with the rest of the Hydrographic Office staff, threw up his hands and said, "We don't know how they could do it so accurately without the airplane." Of course, maybe it wasn't done without an airplane. Remember the discs moving along the coast of Wales as though in search of something? Survey teams?

This extraordinary Piri Reis map led to further conclusions which could be supported by logic if not by physical proof. The conclusions stated that spaceship landings could have been made on earth at least ten thousand years ago. This would tie in very nicely with theories of colonization. It would seem natural to bring in advanced technicians in the first group of settlers; supplies would be brought along next; and then less technically advanced persons would be brought.

But these advance space ships may have experienced any of a variety of difficulties and failed to return, leaving beings of great education and potential among primitives, where they might be regarded as gods or super beings yet forced by the circumstances to accept their lot, possibly interbreeding with the primitives of earth and passing along heritages that may have found their ways into ancient scriptures, ultimately regarded by us as myth. As a final stroke of irony, a lack of discovery on the earth seems to substantiate this theory to a greater degree than any discovery.

Among all the archeological explorations which produced evidences of complex lost civilizations, no discovery has been made which suggests factories, fuel plants, or the laboratories needed to power these ancient UFOs. No scroll or tablet has been discovered to suggest the vaguest possibility that the ancient space craft which may have visited earth were, indeed, of an earthly origin. This lack of adequate machinery and fuel would seem to argue strongly that flying objects, if they did land here at all, came from other points in space.

Much of what has been discussed here is theory of the highest order. But we've had some indication that today's theories can be fairly well-educated guesses.

What do we know for sure? We know that we have thick sheaves of unexplainable incidents, past and present, on our hands. We know that *something* is here. We live in the absolute certainty that there is more to come. We know that we haven't seen anything yet.

CHAPTER SIX

UFOs Galore

Recent Gallup Poll figures show an excess of five million persons in the United States claiming to have seen UFOs. There are no accurate figures on the number of persons who believe these mysterious objects are real, although estimates have been made that over fifteen million people think so. The growing tendency among these people is to suppose that UFOs are of an extraterrestrial nature.

As late as January, 1967, UFOs were still good copy—good enough to merit feature treatment on the cover of *Science & Mechanics,* and through the final months of 1966, *Look* featured a condensation of John G. Fuller's *The Interrupted Journey,* while *Mechanix Illustrated* extracted portions of Fuller's *Incident at Exeter.* As far as *Popular Science* was concerned, UFOs are big business, meriting front-cover treatment.

Since 1947 and the famous *True* magazine report by Major Donald E. Keyhoe, other mass-media magazines have carried the UFO-fact-or-fiction debate to millions of readers and have discovered that a reasonably fresh slant, some pictures (no matter how fuzzy or indistinct), and some accounts of new sightings are good shots in the arm for circulation. In 1966, a book with a borrowed title, written by Frank Edwards, reached the best-seller lists.

In late October, 1966, the American Broadcasting Company, in an hour-long TV special, had some brief, if unencouraging words to say about UFOs. The Air Force grant of $300,000, given to the University of Colorado for an eighteen-month study of UFOs, while it did not displace the war in Viet Nam, managed to get its share of front-page space in newspapers throughout the country.

During the first week in November of 1966, KRLA, a Los Angeles radio station devoted to rock-and-roll records and spot announcements, assured whatever beings listening in whatever UFOs were hovering near earth, that we are eager to see them land, that we are peaceful in our intentions, and that we would love to hear from them. The UFOs were even given a designated spot on the AM radio band on which to make their transmission. There was no response to KRLA's invitation, at least not from UFOs, but ensuing phone-in interviews brought within earshot the conjecture and details of a modern phenomenon to an audience that was not even alive when Kenneth Arnold made his famed 1947 sighting.

Veteran news commentator Frank Edwards, took the title of his best-selling book from an Air Force operations and training special order which said in part: "Unidentified flying objects—sometimes treated lightly by the press and referred to as 'flying saucers'—must be rapidly and accurately identified as serious USAF business . . ." Just how serious the press and radio-TV media really are about UFOs is a matter of some conjecture. But it cannot be denied that these media know a popular subject when they see one.

It is most probable, as a result of such recent UFO public-ity, that an impressive number of persons are at the very least

flying from a point between Boise and Meridian, Idaho. The objects were black in color. They made no sound and neither their speed nor altitude were determined. Rated as an observer of good reliability, the pilot described a series of abrupt, right-angle tactics, then a partial barrel roll, after which it disappeared. Using 8-mm motion picture film, the pilot got about ten seconds worth of activity. Subsequent checking with other National Guard personnel revealed a sighting of the same object, flying in the same kind of tactics.

One of the more intriguing UFO sightings came in the early morning hours of March 23, 1960, when the wife of an Indianapolis, Ind., metallurgist awakened with a sore throat and got out of bed to gargle. Looking out her window into a clear, cloudless sky, she saw a brilliant metallic object flying back and forth. "It was as brilliant as a star, but not a glittery brilliance . . . It flew back and forth. After it went west, it turned and went east. It would go up and down . . . It was kind of like a comet shape." She awakened her husband, who saw the object and said "It looked like it had bars instead of being solid. It was more the size of a lima bean . . . It had somewhat the contour of an old-fashioned kite, but I saw nothing like an exhaust or tail . . . As I looked out the window, looking north, it went through an arc about 90 degrees from above the horizon in a matter of a few seconds."

The Air Force conclusion ruled out the possibility of a satellite because of the direction of motion, which also ruled out the possibility of an aircraft, but not of a balloon. It is also probable, the Air Force concluded, that the witnesses saw a reflected or refracted light which was further distorted by the window screen through which they saw the object. But in the absence of any more positive information, the sighting goes into the bulging unidentified file.

Another Project Bluebook case extends in time from October, 1957, to April 25, 1960, at various hours between 9 P.M. and midnight on a farm near Shelby, Mont. Five sightings were reported by a housewife and farm hand with a reliability rated as fair to good. Each sighting was of approximately twenty minutes duration to a half hour. The UFO was circular or spherical, looking, from the distance it was seen, about the size of a grapefruit held at arm's length, and estimated as 10 feet in diameter. It made no noise but had a red glow within and threw out a strong white light. Speeds ranged from very slow to very fast and the observers estimated the altitude of the objects variously at 50 or 100 feet. The Air Force interrogator said there was probably no accurate way to determine the altitude. The objects always moved in definite lines, made sharp turns, and were able to vary speed from the approximate speed of a man walking to extremely fast. The woman observer made a photograph of the UFOs and sent it to the Project Bluebook headquarters, but Air Force spokesmen said the photos could supply no information that would lead to the establishment of any definite conclusions.

A Kansas City, Kan., aeronautical engineer, his wife, and their two young daughters stayed up late to see the early morning overhead passage of the Echo Satellite on August 23, 1960. They saw the Echo, but they also saw a UFO and ended up as a case history with Project Bluebook. Hold a golfball at arm's length and you'll get an idea of the size the UFO appeared to be in the engineer's description. The sphere, with its three triangular-shaped lights of yellow, gave the appearance of a Japanese lantern. Speculation was raised that the triangular lights, each about one-tenth the size of the total sphere, were lights. No estimate on the UFO's speed was given, but it was placed as very fast as it appeared to fly a pursuit curve on the Echo Satellite. The UFO was in observation for approximately two minutes, but no traces of exhaust trail were noticed. As it appeared to track the Echo Satellite, the UFO held a steady course with no hoverings or power spurts or associated changes of color.

An object that looked very much like the planet Mars, because the planet Mars was right there for comparison, was seen in the sky over Chula Vista, Calif., on November 27, 1960, by two observers of excellent reliability and five others of unknown reliability. Two astronomers, the manager of a trailer court, two housewives, and two other persons saw what was described as follows: An object that "looked like the planet Mars with a very long antenna rod attached; a flashing white light of high intensity ran back and forth along the rod." The UFO made no sound as it moved all over the sky in huge circles. It reportedly made spurts of tremendous speed, raced over the nearby border into the Lower California portion of Mexico, "and then circled some more and then returned and from where we were viewing, it went out over North Island and hovered some more. Kindly remember that seven people (three with binoculars) were viewing this object for a long time. Then it vanished. And did not reappear." The entire sighting took from twenty minutes to half an hour.

Reports show the planet Mars, which was visible in the sky at the time, available for two important comparisons. When the UFO was overhead, it appeared as large as Mars and was almost the same color. When the UFO moved into Mexico it seemed to be the size of the planet Mercury.

"The best way I [the wife of the amateur astronomer, herself an amateur astronomer] can describe it is to say that it was a bit redder than Mars and was describing huge circles in the air . . . it looked like a Fourth of July sparkler connected at the side of the object . . . It was unquestionably some kind of intelligently controlled air or space vehicle." The sharpness of the report given by this couple is emphasized by another Project Bluebook report dated about three and a half months later, and less than twenty miles away, in San Diego, Calif.

Two fighter pilots, attached to the All-Weather Fighter-Interceptor Squadron based on the same North Island over which the amateur astronomers saw their UFO, "were just going home from a routine alert." They saw an unusual light in the sky. When they arrived home, they saw the light still hovering. Thinking the object might be a satellite, they watched for a few moments with naked eye, but when they saw the object was not moving as a satellite would, they got binoculars and watched it. "At first it was almost due east. It seemed to be moving east to west. Then it made a 90-degree turn toward the north. A minute or so later, it turned another 90 degrees and went back east." Both pilots saw the UFO for nearly ten minutes. "What intrigued us was the light from this object. It wasn't the kind of light you see from a reciprocating engine exhaust at night or from a jet afterburner. The nearest you can describe it is to say it looked like a steady stream of electric sparks. Something like a sparkler on the Fourth of July."

There are many similarities between this and the Chula Vista sighting. The Project Bluebook record attempts to rule out the sightings as UFOs by suggesting the possibility of "a refracted astronomical object, but the movement from east to west and the high elevation angle tends to rule out this possibility." Besides, there were at least four highly competent observers who saw the two UFOs through binoculars. Score two more for the Unidentified file.

Another puzzler made an appearance on May 22, 1961, in the skies over Tyndall Air Force Base, Florida. An Air Force wife who saw a silvery disc the size of a volleyball said she had never seen anything like it before, so she told her neighbor, another Air Force wife. For a full fifteen minutes, the two women watched the object as it revolved, hovering at a point about 3½ degrees above the southeast horizon. Suddenly the hovering stopped and the object rose to an angle of about 35 degrees on the horizon before it vanished from sight. In terse fashion, the Air Force allowed that these two women probably had had enough experience to be able to tell a helicopter when they saw it. Thus, their hovering disc was added to the ranks of unidentifiable flying objects.

Wherever possible, Project Bluebook reports are not considered complete until the witness or witnesses supply rough drawings of the object or objects they have seen. A pair of students, both seniors at Drake University, have produced a drawing of a huge object, "slightly less than half the size of a football field," sighted by them for a period of three to five minutes in Kansas City on August 12, 1961. The object bears a strong resemblance to Capt. Jim Hooton's strange object of 1897. The Kansas City monster UFO was described as "like a huge oval or bobsled shape with lighted automobile-type 'running boards' along the outer edges; also had a high vertical tail, circular in shape, which ran from one edge to center of object."

It is an almost certain corollary that Project Bluebook sightings such as this will be fed into computers for matching against future sightings, along with a special coding for the reliability of the witness. In a way, it seems a shame that Capt.

Hooton must be cheated of his fair time on the computers, but perhaps current sightings of the behemoth UFOs will pile up a neater argument in his favor.

While Capt. Hooton's UFO made a sound that was similar to a Westinghouse air brake, this one was silent, capable of great speed and sureness of movement. The observers saw it hovering at an altitude of about 50 feet above a road. Then it moved straight up and climbed rapidly away on a sharp eastern heading. Air Force comment: "Weather was clear and dry. No wind, no weather inversions in the area were reported by meteorologists. The observers were driving along a road in a convertible with the top down." The Air Force classified this incident as unknown. They say portions of the description indicate the possibility of the UFO being a balloon, but the altitude of 50 feet at the time of sighting and the description of the sudden rising seem to be sufficient enough to preclude any further balloon theories.

In Washington, D.C., an ex-Navy pilot and flight instructor, a most reliable witness, and two other men sighted a UFO from two different locations. The descriptions of all three men jibe with the exception that the ex-Navy pilot went into more technical details.

As an interesting clue on how the classification game works in these instances, the noiseless, dark-grey, diamond-shaped object about 20 feet long was classified as unidentified. If the UFO with a pulsating orange-brown glow in "approximately one-third of the center area" had been an experimental craft belonging to the Air Force, Army, or Navy, it would immediately have been given a secret classification and the chances are, no information would have been released.

William J. Meyer, Jr., the ex-pilot, said of his sighting: "At no time while I had the object in view did it change course or altitude, or move behind or in front of something and reappear . . . The motion was smooth and speed seemed constant. The orange-brown glow in the center portion seemed to pulse at rather a rapid rate . . . As the object passed directly over my head, I saw that it was diamond shaped . . . I estimated the object to be between 1200 and 1500 feet above me . . . I am convinced that the object I saw was as I have described it and could not have been any conventional heavier- or lighter-than-air craft, any phenomenon caused by temperature inversion mirage, or sun reflection . . . I have not been able to reconcile what I saw with any known object which would give any similar likeness if put in the air." This sighting was made on December 13, 1961.

Six observers at Blandford, Mass., saw something that looked like "a red diamond with slightly rounded edges" on May 26, 1962. The UFO was about the apparent size of the sun, and gave off sparks like a Fourth of July sparkler, a description that is beginning to sound more common. Duration of sighting was approximately five minutes. From the moment at which it was first noticed, the object described a gentle S-curve descent, moving out of sight behind trees. The observers thought it might have landed on a mountain, but soon after reaching this conclusion, they saw it distinctly airborne again. The observers did not see the object vanish. They left while it was still visible to them. At no time during the sighting did the object appear to be going faster than 100 miles an hours. The observer reliability is indeterminate, but the Air Force says the object could not have been a refracted image of the sun from below the horizon. The lateness of the hour—11:45 P.M.—prevented that possibility.

Nearly a year to the day later, a fifteen-year-old New

Zealand college boy made the list when he thought he heard the wail of an animal on a nearby hillside. Looking up from his campsite where he was alone, the boy saw instead a blurred, semidisc object that was moving between the camp and a mountainside. The UFO was an estimated 60 feet in diameter. As the young camper watched it, the disc suddenly made a 270-degree turn and moved away, curving back in the direction from which it came.

With his sighting of a whitish, egg-shaped UFO about the size of a sedan, Socorro, N.M., policeman Lonnie Zamora made the Project Bluebook list as an observer of good reliability. In addition to noticing the insignia already described in chapter two, officer Zamora claimed to see actual persons in connection with his incident. The sighting began when officer Zamora was chasing a speeding auto, saw what looked like a bright flash, and decided this might have been a dynamite shack going up. He drove out into the New Mexico desert to investigate. In transit, he saw a flash of flame and color, then heard a roar that changed from high to low frequency, then stopped. Moving in the direction of the noise and flames, he came upon a deserted stretch of road on which he thought to find the dynamite shack or some possible accident.

"Suddenly," he said, "I noted a shiny-type object to the south . . . It looked at first like a car turned upside down . . . Saw two people in white coveralls very close to the object. One of these persons seemed to turn and look straight at my car and seemed startled—seemed to quickly jump somewhat . . . These persons appeared normal in shape—but possibly they were small adults or large kids." Officer Zamora paid attention to the road while driving closer to the scene. He stopped his car then and radioed to Socorro to alert the Sheriff's office for a possible accident. While using his microphone, he heard a roar, "a very loud roar . . . The flame was under the object. The object was starting to go straight up—slowly up. Flame was light blue and at the bottom it was sort of an orange color . . . The object was smooth—no windows or doors visible. As roar started, it was still on or near the ground." At this point, Officer Zamora noticed the strange insignia or markings on the side of the craft. He kept the craft in sight for a few moments longer as the noises it emitted trailed off sharply. The object was then in motion, traveling swiftly up and suddenly away.

Officer Zamora's UFO was not tracked on the radar screen at the nearby Holloman Air Force Base and one reason for this was given as the possibility that it was deliberately keeping at a low level as it flew in. After carefully going through Zamora's story, no information was obtained that even remotely suggested a vehicle such as the one seen. The Air Force placed this sighting in the category of a good unknown.

Three high school boys in Urbana, Ohio, said they were willing to take a police department lie detector test as a proof of their sincerity when they made a UFO report on August 30, 1965. Their reliability as observers is rated good for their report that a large, solid ball, trailing a streak of light seemed to come straight down out of the sky, strike the road and bounce straight back up again until it was out of sight. The entire sighting took less than five seconds, suggesting that the UFO was moving at a tremendous speed. The ball did not seem to illuminate the surrounding area, but the boys who saw it said it was "awfully bright."

On September 3, 1965, at about two in the morning, the now famous Exeter incident occurred about 3 miles from the small New Hampshire town situated close to the Massachusetts border. The early characters were Norman Muscarello, a young man three weeks away from joining the Navy, Exeter policeman Reginald Toland, and Exeter policeman Eugene Bertrand.

Entering the Exeter station where young Muscarello was still shaken and nervous, patrolman Bertrand told a strange story. He had come across a lone woman parked by the side of the road, and obviously making a tremendous struggle to retain her composure. When Bertrand questioned her, she said that a huge, silent object had been hovering only a few feet from her car, staying with her from the town of Epping, a scant 12 miles away. As she reached an overpass, the UFO took off at a tremendous burst of speed and seemed to disappear among the stars. Patrolman Toland turned to the young Norman Muscarello with more of a believing look now. "Does this sound like your thing?" Muscarello nodded emphatically. This was a very close description of the thing that had been very close to him, not an hour before.

The UFO seen by Muscarello and the woman found its way into Project Bluebook reports with this description: Five lights close together in a row that was tilted about 60 degrees to the landscape; each was round. The lights moved over a large field and sometimes fluttered to a lower altitude in a maneuver that resembled a falling leaf; they repeatedly descended behind houses and trees and then reappeared after an interval of time. The Air Force says these lights were bright enough to cast a red glow over the surrounding landscape. The lights flashed in sequence, from one to another along the row. After the final flash of the last object in the row, the sequence would be repeated in reverse, beginning with the last ball and moving down to the first. At times, these lights settled so low that they seemed to be settling to the ground or possibly attacking the observers. The Exeter sighting was so dramatic that John G. Fuller, a noted columnist for

The Saturday Review of Literature was motivated to write a book-length investigation.

Project Bluebook files appear to be rather sketchy on the March, 1966, sighting over Benton Harbor, Mich., and perhaps this is because their investigations are not yet completed. Nevertheless, three rubbish collectors, a policeman, and the news director of a radio station gave reports—some contradictory—that presented a frankfurter-shaped object which may have been fifteen stories high. The rubbish collectors said the object was so bright that it was difficult to look at. The news director said it was the color of a star and had red and green lights. Other details were sketchy.

On March 23, 1966, a lone, unidentified male driver was on a main highway near Temple, Okla. The time, 5:05 A.M. Because of the details given in his report, Bluebook rates the observer as fairly reliable. He saw an object like a conventional aircraft but without wings or engines. It had a bubble canopy but no wheels. Nevertheless, it was resting on some kind of support. Imagine the driver's surprise. He encountered the UFO parked on the highway. The observer stopped his car, got out, and started walking toward the object. He saw a man wearing a baseball cap enter the UFO by steps from the bottom. Then, almost immediately, the UFO rose and headed southeast at a reported speed of sound. An Air Force check revealed that there were no experimental or conventional craft in the area at that time. Although several helicopters and experimental craft are located nearby, none could be placed even remotely near the area of sighting at the time of sighting.

These are all sightings that have puzzled Project Bluebook. These are the ones they cannot ignore or write off as balloons, freaks of weather, or experimental aircraft. These are the ones they want to know about the most. Perhaps the public has some reason for complaint over past Air Force policies of appearing to hedge or downgrade UFO reports. But the fact that Project Bluebook is interested in these sightings and others like them is some indication for hope. We might find out what's going on, after all. And it's some consolation to note that even if your own personal favorite of the hundreds of UFO sightings does not land on the Project Bluebook list, there are still plenty of strange, unexplainable sightings, unique and intriguing, undergoing investigation.

CHAPTER SEVEN

Foes of UFOs

Walter Sullivan, science editor of the New York *Times* finds it difficult to believe that intelligent life does not exist on other planets, although he doesn't think we will find this kind of life in other parts of our own solar system, and he is especially convinced that UFOs are not the so-called flying saucers.

"Many serious and intelligent people have seen things," Sullivan said, "and you can't just dismiss them as cranks." But he believes the theory of UFOs being interplanetary space craft is, at best, a specious argument. "The problem with visitors from outer space is a simple and logical one. It's not possible to travel faster than the speed of light, so if intelligent life from other solar systems were to visit us, it would take at least two hundred years to make the trip. Now after traveling for that amount of time, are you just going to buzz a few swamps and then leave?"

An intelligent critic realizes he is rarely in a position to insist that his is the only possible point of view and that an opposing argument is impossible. Mr. Sullivan wisely admits that he won't say flying saucers are "absolutely impossible, but I reviewed all those saucer books for the *Times Book Review*, and if you ask me, they're all pretty silly."

Mr. Sullivan has also written a book, *We Are Not Alone,*

and because of the increased interest in the possibility of life on other planets, UFOs, the theories of an expanding universe, and other related phenomena, Mr. Sullivan was called upon to revise his 1964 edition. Undoubtedly, this newest edition will focus on the possibilities of life-supporting atmospheres far out beyond earth, hundreds and possibly millions of lightyears away. He represents an excellent example of a highly informed, literate person, intrigued with the possibilities of space and discovery, taking a pragmatic point of view and cautiously watching developments to see what happens. Mr. Sullivan is just the sort of critic UFO buffs need to keep them firmly anchored to the realm of the possible when the tendency is to let wishful thinking take over.

Another articulate spokesman on the UFO phenomena is Dr. Phillip Morrison, a physicist at Massachusetts Institute of Technology. Dr. Morrison says, "It [the UFO] is a social phenomenon, a phenomenon of journalism and television. If you look in the newspapers and journals of a hundred or a hundred and twenty years ago, you'll see the same thing— exactly the same thing. They're much more frequent now, but most of the things they [the UFO sighters] see, as we all well know, are aircraft, lights in the sky, planets, and so on." Dr. Morrison contends that many of the UFO observers are just not well enough versed in science to be able to cope with what they see in any other way than the invention of the flying saucer. He says that the flying saucers are, of course, possible, but they are far less probable than anything else we know about science.

Dr. Morrison also attributes the tendency to secrecy, well defined over the past twenty-five or thirty years, as a causative factor. With so many projects and devices being given government or service priorities and security ratings, the uninformed public is more likely to think that something momentous is being withheld from them. The residue, he says, "is a lot of new and interesting phenomena which would be quite nice to have explained." But Dr. Morrison's belief is that there are many more things of interest and value to discover, and he is willing to let the flying saucer stay on the books as a social and periodic phenomenon that creeps up now and then.

In the main, scientists tend to be quite careful in ruling out the possibilities that UFOs = flying saucers = interplanetary travelers. Most, even though they don't think much of the connection between UFOs and interplanetary visitors, try to leave themselves a way out of committing themselves absolutely to a thing they cannot disprove any more than we can prove.

One top scientist in the aerospace industry in California asked to remain nameless even though he took a rather cautious point of view. "It amazes me," he said, "how many engineers, chemists, physicists, pilots, and the like suddenly drop their objectivity the minute they make a sighting. Every time you read about a UFO sighting by one of these persons, you always get that little pat argument of how they were firm skeptics until they saw something. After they've had their experience, they buy the whole package. UFOs are real, they really come from outer space, and they're manned by superintelligent beings.

"I say that a man who calls himself a scientist is serving notice that he is devoting his career to observing the unknown, and if some of these people, on the strength of what I'll freely admit is an amazing, frightening, out-of-the-ordinary experience, are willing to throw away their credentials without further proof, then in my book, they're giving up the right to call themselves scientists. Just because a doctor sees something unusual in a set of symptoms, he doesn't throw everything he's learned out the front door and consult an African witch doctor.

"We know there's something there, we know it's strange, but we don't know what it is, period."

While not a scientist, Andrew Tackaberry has spent hundreds of hours aloft as a jet pilot of photo reconnaissance planes for the Air Force. He has also had extensive experience in writing reports and operational documents according to rigorous governmental specifications. Author of *Famous Ghosts, Phantoms, and Poltergeists for the Millions,* and books on ESP subjects, Tackaberry says he would like to be able to reconcile his interest in psychical research with some of the prevalent UFO theories. But he finds this position rather difficult.

"I've seen many convincing reflections and atmospheric phenomena," he said. "These are as diversified as your UFOs and often just as convincing. On one particular flight, I became quite irritated with the man on my right. I thought he was maintaining formation a bit too tightly, and I gave him hell over the intercom, but I had to apologize when I realized it was a very realistic reflection of my ship, bouncing off a cloud formation."

Tackaberry thinks there may be some strange phenomena sighted, but this does not come close to making them manned craft or interplanetary ships.

One of the most famous of all names connected with UFOs is a Harvard University astronomer, Dr. Donald Menzel. The eventual subject of attack or snide remarks from nearly every serious author on the subject of flying saucers, Dr. Menzel has patiently tried to debunk the major UFO sightings as optical illusions, atmospheric conditions, balloons, conventional aircraft, and other standard situations. It is almost a corollary that if you have any positive feelings about UFOs, you have to prove your worth by taking a crack at Dr. Menzel. In the next chapter, we'll meet some of his most ardent detractors, and get some idea why this careful scientist has made such an impression in the UFO community, but for the moment, let's take a closer look at some of his theories.

At the very beginning of his "scientific examination of a major myth of the space age," Dr. Menzel links the flying saucer myth to Charles Fort, a talented reporter and author and a great distruster of orthodox knowledge because "he believed it smugly damned to oblivion all reports of marvels that it could not explain: pyrogenic persons, rains of fish, frogs, and stones; accounts of telepathy, teleportation, the vanishing of human beings, luminous objects in the sky."

Fort enjoyed collecting such accounts and using them to challenge scientists for explanations of things which seemed to defy explanation. As a sample of Charles Fort: "Unknown, luminous things, or beings, have often been seen, sometimes close to this earth, and sometimes high in the sky. It may be that some of them were living things that occasionally came from somewhere in our existence, but that others were lights on the vessels of explorers, or voyagers, from somewhere else."

Menzel attributes this Fortean influence and the tremendous impact of science fiction magazines and of the psychically oriented *Fate* magazine to conditioning the public to believe in flying saucers.

On the matter of the tragic death of Capt. Mantell that we saw in the chapter on classic sightings, we have Dr. Menzel's theory that the object in chase was not a spacecraft at all but rather a "mock sun," tiny crystals of ice which float in a layer of quiet air. A thin layer of these crystals might well be

81

invisible to the observer, but sunlight filtering through such a layer of ice crystals may reflect a pattern of bright spots in the sky. Sometimes this reflected pattern of spots appears to be brighter than the sun itself. The resulting phenomenon is called a sun dog. Similar results may be had from the reflection of the moon on these ice crystals. These are called moon dogs.

Dr. Menzel's original theory about the Mantell death involved a sun dog, but this was amended in 1963 by the disclosure that the Clinton County Air Force Base in southern Ohio had been a launching site for the famed Skyhook balloons. Records for the day of Mantell's death are not available, and no one at the base can remember if a Skyhook balloon had been launched that day, but Dr. Menzel says the records at Wright-Patterson Field show that winds that day would have carried a balloon exactly over the course Mantell followed while chasing his UFO. In Menzel's words, "without the Skyhook records for the day in question, this solution cannot be called absolutely certain. But the chances of its being correct are overwhelmingly high—infinitely higher than the probability that Mantell died while chasing a spaceship from another planet."

Retired Marine Major Donald Keyhoe did not like Dr. Menzel's sun dog theory. "Though Menzel did not say so, he implied that all the other witnesses were likewise deluded [as deluded by the mock sun theory as Mantell was]." Keyhoe did not like the Skyhook balloon possibility either. But why stop there? Keyhoe didn't like Menzel's answer to an unsolved 1948 spaceship sighting by Eastern Air Lines pilots. His proposition that the witnesses were misled by a mirage which was caused by layers of hot and cold air did not wash with the terrierlike Keyhoe. And Keyhoe virtually throws up his hands at Dr. Menzel's explanation of the Lt. George Gorman incident over Fargo, S.D. Again illusion, Menzel said, only a light reflection from a distance, caused by a whirlpool of air over the fighter wingtip.

The critics of Dr. Menzel—Keyhoe among them—claim that the Harvard astronomer takes the closest possible scientific theories and tries to apply them *in toto* to UFO sightings, whether they are truly applicable or not. But other scientists say this is normal procedure and that it has led to most of the valuable discoveries in many disciplines. Another of Dr. Menzel's techniques is to take a series of statements accepted as fact, show them as not being fact, then demonstrate how these misstatements have been jumbled into false conclusions.

A good example is his discussion of meteors. The frequent sightings of fireballs in the sky—many of them green—behaving "in ways that meteors don't behave," gave the astronomer a field day. He noted five false premises after making the rather acid comment that green fireballs still appear just as they always have. "None of them has yet changed into a spaceship."

The first of the five false premises about meteors is that they do not contain copper. From this false premise is based the notion that the green color of the sighted fireballs could only come from copper and must, therefore, be spacecraft because they could not be meteors.

Another false premise exploded by Dr. Menzel: meteors do not travel at slow rates of speed and do not maintain a horizontal path. Since the green fireballs did both, they must not be meteors but spacecraft. Dr. Menzel says meteors do travel at slow speeds and do follow horizontal paths on occasion and, therefore, the fireballs don't necessarily have to be spacecraft.

Third: Meteors do not show as great a size or brilliance as

the reported fireballs, therefore the fireballs must not be meteors, they must be spacecraft. Not true, the doctor says. Meteors can show as much size and brilliance as the green fireballs.

Fourth: Meteors produce a loud noise. Since the huge green fireballs moved silently, they were not meteors but spacecraft. Again, the doctor turns thumbs down and says "Most meteors silently vaporize above earth." But he points out that some meteors, as they rush through the air, do make noises which have been described as weak hissing, rumbling, etc.

The final matter is one of fragments. All meteors deposit fragments on earth, the fallacy says. And since the green fireballs left no fragments, they must be spacecraft. Dr. Menzel says most meteors burn up high in the atmosphere, and even if some of the body does survive to reach the surface of the earth, finding it presents a gigantic problem. Recovery, he says, is rare even when the fall occurs in daylight over well-populated country and the flight path can be charted from the accounts of reliable witnesses or tracking stations.

Among the many fireball episodes Dr. Menzel used his five points to debunk were those sighted on September 20, 1955. One particular batch was seen that night in a six-state area. They were seen from aloft by plane crews. The fireballs vanished without trace. Other vanishing fireballs alluded to by Menzel were seen on various occasions between 1950 and 1955.

How, the reader might ask, can a man be so sure of himself even when he admits we don't know all the answers to the UFO enigma? The answer is that Dr. Menzel is by no means so sure, he is simply trying to use observable facts and information as a standard against which to judge the UFO sightings.

In the past, the reliability of one or more witnesses was never at issue. But how can we be sure, absolutely sure of what they were seeing? Their reports might have been accurate in every detail—as far as they went. Their reports may have been as honest as humanly possible, but lacking in important data.

Well, then, what does it take? What is the proof required to convince men such as Dr. Menzel? Simple enough, we have to have a UFO on the ground at close range so that experts in at least two different fields can thump it, tap it, photograph it, and crawl under it. We have to have a contact with any beings that might be inside the craft, a contact that lasts longer than just a few minutes, a contact that is made by persons who are close to the aliens—if there are, in fact, any aliens—in ability, understanding, and education.

For all the sincerity and dedication shown by persons who have claimed to hold conversations with these alien "space people," we have to have a more conclusive communication with much more detailed answers. And we need some indication of why, if many of the UFO sightings really are alien spacecraft, some attempt at a conclusive contact has not been made earlier. Until then, maddening and slow-paced as it might seem, we should anchor some part of our imaginations to the issues raised by men like Dr. Menzel. In the meanwhile, as a sort of scientific bone thrown to us: the strong suspicions that there is some form of intelligent life on other planets and the intriguing assurances that some experiments are being made along the lines of attempts to send and receive radio contact with other likely inhabited planets.

And Dr. Menzel will attempt to punch holes in the more likely sounding UFO reports. Let's have another look at him in action as he reviews another incident we've encountered earlier. This is what he has to say about the Nash–Fortenberry incident over the Chesapeake Bay.

In this sighting, pilots Nash and Fortenberry saw a staggered formation of discs appear to flip up on end and abruptly reverse their course while moving at a tremendous rate of speed. "The extraterrestrial conclusion depends even more strongly on the . . . assumption that the UFOs were material objects. Nearly every part of the description is in conflict with this idea. The instantaneous reversal of course, for example, if performed by solid objects, should have produced shock waves that would have broken windows in Norfolk, Newport News, and points west. Only one observation even suggests that the unknowns had a material nature: when the discs flipped on edge they seemed to reveal bottom surfaces, which would indicate a solid body. The witnesses specifically qualified this statement, however, by adding that though they had the impression that the bottom surfaces were unlighted, the 'bottoms' were not clearly visible. Thus the three-dimensional structure was not actually observed but only inferred."

For more probable causes than extraterrestrial origin, Dr. Menzel discarded the possibility that the planet Mercury, the only planet that could have been involved, was not in the picture. He also investigated the possibility of multiple reflections in the window, but accepted the "overwhelming probability that the source of the UFOs was outside and below the aircraft." The probable cause of the Nash–Fortenberry incident was then ascribed to beacon lights, shining on cloud bottoms.

Before leaving Dr. Menzel, one more bit of information seems particularly interesting in light of his comments about Charles Fort and science fiction being greatly responsible for our current attitudes and beliefs about UFOs. The doctor, himself, is an admitted science fiction buff, and spends some of his leisure time writing it. Exit, for the moment, one very dedicated, determined scientist, bending over backwards to pin UFOs down to being real events. But the doctor will be back from time to time to plague us.

Meanwhile, let's look at a brilliant young scientist who seems to agree with Dr. Morrison that intelligent life may be found on other planets, but who has a very telling point to make about one particular phase of UFO sightings. Dr. Carl Sagan is an assistant professor of astronomy at Harvard University and a staff member of the Smithsonian Astrophysical Observatory in Cambridge, Mass. Dr. Sagan notes that New Mexico, particularly the areas near the White Sands Proving Grounds, has been a rich source of UFO sightings.

Between the years of 1954 and 1958, Dr. Sagan reminds us, the Harvard Meteor Project was in full force and extensive observations were made by Super-Schmidt cameras with a 60-degree field of view. Over an intensive period of more than three thousand hours, a wide-spread viewing operation was performed by men with excellent equipment that made photographic observations of other phenomena down to a magnitude of +4, which is closely related to the faintest object visible with the naked eye. In addition, here were trained professionals, actively seeking moving objects. During this study, not one picture was taken of anything resembling a UFO, yet during the time of the study, UFO reports in the area were plentiful.

Dr. Sagan leaves us with a very big and very cogent, why not?

Shortly after the Air Force realized it held a tiger by the tail in matters of UFOs, it found the tiger becoming more and more energetic. Large segments of the public began to think, and still do, that the Air Force was and is deliberately holding back information. The more avid of UFO fans can show how the source of official attitude described by the Air Force between the years of 1947 and 1967 is every bit as erratic as the course of the most bizarre sighting yet recorded.

One reason why the Air Force seems to have behaved in so suspicious a manner is because it was of at least two minds in the matter of which position to take. Another reason is because it is a chain-of-command type of organization which must follow the policy that is set, even if that policy is to be changed. A third reason, the potential for turnover of key personnel and the requests made of these key people by other high government and military figures.

As an official act, the Air Force was among the very first to suggest that all UFO sightings had some neat, tidy resolution. As further official acts, the Air Force seemed to go out of its way to support this position and to require the same, unwavering behavior of all its men. The Air Force also seemed to be holding back on information, cutting off further reports on a new sighting and, when there was some news leak, saying the matter had been officially solved. Accordingly, the Air Force has found itself, from time to time, with much the same reputation as Dr. Menzel, with one difference; Dr. Menzel asked for the UFOs, the Air Force got them whether they wanted it or not.

As the number of sightings began to increase, off-the-record Air Force statements began to indicate that they believed there was more to flying saucers than met the eye. For this very reason, statements concerning the UFOs and possible conclusions which might be made from them were handled in a cautious, circumspect manner. Already, national magazines were breaking stories that had a curious nation clamoring for more, and the Air Force found itself in a position of not knowing what to tell them. If they told too much, they were accused of spreading panic; if they seemed to be holding back, they weren't telling the truth.

One Air Force major, connected with public information but not specifically with Project Bluebook or any other UFO information-gathering group, was approached for the most general of comments for this book. The major was asked if the Air Force had had recent reason to take on a more positive attitude toward UFOs. His response was terse and no-nonsense. UFOs, he said, were strictly crack-pot stuff.

Was it true, he was asked, that Air Force personnel were given blanket instructions not to make comments about the possibilities that UFOs were really interplanetary craft? This time, the reply was a terse "No comment." The subject was changed.

In fairness to the major and to the Air Force, no specific request of the major was made that he contact Project Bluebook, even for so much as the latest press handout. And within a month after the major was questioned, Project Bluebook released data on previously unpublicized sightings and findings. Recent indications show that the Air Force is more than willing to cooperate by making available to responsible persons the very cases which are presenting the most problems.

From past performance records, the Air Force must go down on record as being foes of the people who want more detailed information about UFOs and who want to believe UFOs are manned and unmanned vehicles from other worlds. But there is another side of the ledger, one that has recently shown the Air Force deciding to cooperate by showing their most difficult cases to the public and because they have put something in the pot: time, effort, men, and money.

Another of these very borderline cases is a man who very

aptly fits in toward the end of this chapter and the beginning of the next. Dr. H. Allen Hynek, Chairman of the Dearborn Observatory at Northwestern University and Scientific Consultant on UFOs to the Air Force, has found himself in a position where he could easily take over as the new Dr. Menzel.

When the now famous March, 1966, sightings took place over Michigan, newspapers raised the familiar hue and cry, a United States Congressman demanded a full Congressional investigation, and some commentators made it appear as if "the truth" were about to be made public at last. Dr. Hynek calmly made a statement that caused all hell to break loose. He said many of the Michigan sightings could have been caused by a phenomenon called *ignis fatuus,* or swamp gas. But because his official release was taken slightly out of context, Dr. Hynek was jumped on for trying to hide the truth, for "parroting the same old Air Force line," and for trying to belittle those who believed in UFOs.

Actually, Dr. Hynek's most direct statement about UFOs is that he neither believes nor disbelieves in their existence but is looking for further evidence from which to make a conclusion. He has said that he thinks "a dismal swamp is a most unlikely place for a visit from outer space." And he was careful to emphasize his belief that not all the Michigan saucer sightings of 1966 were the result of swamp or marsh gas. Even so, his statement about the swamp gas brought forth angry retorts, particularly from UFO fan magazines. In addition, there were reports that when UFO sightings were made over some swampy areas, the atmospheric conditions were so windy that the spontaneous combustion conditions of swamp fire were not present.

Dr. Hynek is probably one of the fairest persons connected

with drawing inferences about individual UFO cases from the available material. If you read on at any great length about future sightings, Dr. Hynek is sure to be a name you'll encounter. And if he seems to be a foe of UFOs at times, do remember that the cases on which he throws up his hands in despair are more likely to be those that will be the most convincing.

And if, at times, such men as Dr. Hynek seem to get on your nerves with their conservative, nit-picking approach, remember another foe of another widely popular cause. Refusing to be backed into a hurried decision, Dr. Frances Kelsey was almost single-handedly responsible for preventing the introduction into this country of the drug thalidomide. Already popular in Europe, the drug had had great publicity and many women in this country were clamoring for it. But Dr. Kelsey's insistence that the drug was unsafe was later proved to be quite warranted, and untold thousands of unborn babies were spared the potential of facing life as cripples or without one or more limbs.

With the possible exception of the American scientist and author Isaac Asimov, Arthur C. Clarke is unique in the field of writing intelligently, knowingly, and interestingly about topics related to space and space travel. To be sure, there are other excellent writers in the field, but both Dr. Asimov and Arthur C. Clarke seem to be able to turn off the straight-fact writing at will and produce extremely high-grade fiction based on the latest or most plausible scientific foundations. Both men have already poured a distinguished bulk of science fiction onto the market, winning awards for imagination, for accuracy, and for quality.

With several highly regarded novels about space travel to his credit, Arthur C. Clarke would seem a natural to be an enthusiastic believer in the theory that UFOs are solid, dimensional objects, capable of interstellar flight. But Clarke has made his position quite clear with the comment: "The working rule for UFO observers is this: it's not a spaceship unless you can read the Mars registration plate."

Astonished by the extreme interest in UFOs, Clarke says the question and answer periods of his lectures are devoted almost equally between discussions of UFOs and all other objects. And he makes one point which is a striking rebuttal to those who claim they can no longer pass off UFOs lightly because so many have been seen. Clarke says he's seen too many reports of UFOs that have turned out to be not something incredible, but something unfamiliar.

By no means as firm or emphatic in his refutations as Dr. Menzel, Clarke nevertheless has painted himself into a corner with his stand, and is probably closer to believing, as Dr. Morrison does, that UFOs are a social phenomenon.

The best present indications are that eighteen months and $300,000 later, the Air Force-sponsored study at the University of Colorado will produce nothing more conclusive than a record of more modern sightings and a more vividly worded statement that many of the UFOs are real, all right, but real *what*? The resulting volume of findings will sell—if it is published—as well as the controversial Warren Report, and probably cause just as many angry retorts and cries of a massive cover-up.

But maybe by then, men like Dr. Phillip Morrison will have made discoveries of their own, discoveries which will at least cause them to think UFOs are less a social phenomenon and more of a physical phenomenon. Perhaps Dr. Menzel will have a few more scientific explanations that will ruffle the feathers of UFO fans. And perhaps there will be some group or combinations of groups which will make possible another eighteen months of study and another $300,000 budget, and some better answers.

CHAPTER EIGHT

Friends of UFOs

Many of the most ardent believers that UFOs are actual, physical phenomena still don't think their point of origin is extraterrestrial; they blame them on the Russians. But that's all right, the Russians have had their share of bludza (UFO) sightings and some of them are quite willing to think of flying saucers as the result of a decadent Capitalist plot.

There are no figures available on the number of Americans who think UFOs are Russian in origin, but as the space race with that country progresses, the Russians are categorized along with swamp gas, weather balloons, meteors, and other more conventional explanations offered. This is just one of the many types of bedfellows the serious UFO believer finds himself with.

Based on some abortive experiments made by the United States and Canadian governments, the Russian theory, while not a complete impossibility, works out mathematically to be less likely a prospect than the interstellar theory. As an example, there is the ill-fated Avro disc, a man-made flying saucer that barely lifted 4 feet from the ground, then overheated because of engine strain. Nevertheless, some will believe only what they want to believe, and the Russians are as likely a source as any.

One of the most dynamic friends of the UFO has not always felt their motives were friendly, even though he is on record in several places as ardently hoping so. A retired Marine Corps major, a graduate of Annapolis, and Director of the National Investigations Committee on Aerial Phenomena, Donald E. Keyhoe is balding at the forehead, has a military crop to his hair, and seems always to be speaking in sentences that end with exclamation points or question marks.

Using some of his Naval Academy friendships to dig, scrape, pester, and probe closely guarded material from the appropriate military personnel, Keyhoe has constantly held the position that the public has a right to know all there is to be known about UFOs and incidents involving them. To that end, he has pushed doggedly for the declassification of material he considered important. He has commented on UFO incidents at great length in three informative books, *Flying Saucers from Outer Space* (1953), *The Flying Saucer Conspiracy* (1955), and *Flying Saucers: Top Secret* (1960). From the moment *True* magazine editor Ken Purdy signed Major Keyhoe to do an article, "Flying Saucers Have Landed" in the late 1940's, the world of UFOdom has had a champion who would not be silenced. In the main, Keyhoe believes that UFOs are interplanetary, that they have landed on earth on several occasions, and that they may easily be manned by intelligent beings who have not yet chosen to make a large-scale contact.

One of Major Keyhoe's arguments to support his belief that the pilots of these UFOs are reluctant to make contact is the possibility of a language barrier. Another potential reason he offers is that of fear and mistrust.

In a well-dramatized scene from one of his books written in 1960, Major Keyhoe presents a conversation he had with

Frank Edwards, a newscaster, great believer in UFOs and, ultimately, author of his own book, *Flying Saucers—Serious Business*. In the Keyhoe book, he and Edwards, both convinced the world has been under observation for some time, arrive at an educated guess of when that surveillance might have begun. They chose the year 1760. Both men immediately become concerned at the number of wars, including two world wars, these outer space monitors would have seen. Thus Major Keyhoe's potential theory that we are not as attractive as we might be to the bystander.

The National Investigations Committee on Aerial Phenomena (NICAP), of which Keyhoe is director, is located at 1536 Connecticut Avenue, Washington, D.C. It publishes a newspaper, the *UFO Investigator*, of which Dr. Menzel says, "Many of the items printed . . . are based on incomplete evidence."

The major returns the favor by showing how the ATIC does not accept as by any means conclusive the solutions produced by Dr. Menzel in the case of single incidents or in longer and more theoretical reports enveloping many UFO sightings. The Keyhoe–Menzel running battle deserves the description of classic in relation to UFO lore. Following it alone will take the newcomer through many fascinating byways and possibilities of explanations.

In a well-publicized and equally well-dissected incident, Major Keyhoe appeared on a nationwide television documentary program some years back, when the UFO interest had flared to a high point. The subject of the documentary was the UFO, and when the peppery major began to speak, hundreds of thousands of listeners began to move forward on the edges of their seats. Keyhoe has this ability in his speaking and his written accounts. A good percentage of these hundreds of thousands probably thought something was wrong with their TV sets. The audio suddenly "gave out" before the major had spoken too many words.

The problem: Keyhoe was not too happy about the line he had been asked to take. Technicians in the control booth, on signal from directors, switched off the audio in the earnest belief that Keyhoe had deliberately switched from his planned comments. There was great fear that Keyhoe would cause panic. Whether or not he would was academic, although this has been one of Keyhoe's concerns for some time. Although some persons, when they heard this reason for the audio switch off, thought Keyhoe probably had it coming to him, the fact is that it could not have served his purpose better.

Thousands of listeners became seriously interested in what had been a borderline novelty to them. Flying saucers, as they were then called, seemed to be a freak, a matter of momentary interest in an age filled with atomic subs, Sputniks, and wonder drugs. This interference was all the proof they needed that Major Keyhoe was being silenced because he knew too much . . . and might tell. This was proof that flying saucers were real.

Only Major Keyhoe's most severe critics will infer that he is trading on fear and panic. Far from intending to be a rumor monger, his message seems to be that a better educated public will be better equipped to handle whatever the UFOs have to offer in the future. Nevertheless, his findings, his discoveries that have been pried loose, always seem quite dramatic because the major does not trade on the ordinary, run-of-the-mill UFO sighting. One example of Keyhoe in action is the dismay and amazement shown by him when he learned of a dramatic 1956 sighting.

A Navy four-engine Super-Constellation was en route from

a flight across the Atlantic Ocean, its destination the Naval Air Station at Patuxent, Md., with a fueling stop at Gander, Newfoundland. Outside of Gander, flying through a clear night with unlimited visibility, the pilot saw a cluster of lights which he took to be a small city below. Checking with the navigator, the pilot realized they'd have to be considerably off course if the lights below were, indeed, a city. The theory then changed; the lights were other aircraft. But pilot and copilot quickly realized these could be no ordinary aircraft. Since he was carrying four full flight crews in the passenger compartment, the pilot banked closer to the cluster of lights and alerted the other crew men for a consultation.

Just as the Super-Constellation began its circling movement, the mysterious lights dimmed and several colored rings appeared, spreading out through the sky. Of these rings, one appeared to be increasing in size and moving closer. The pilot, bewildered by this strange result, moved from his turn into a full-power climb but quickly noted how useless a gesture that would be. The luminous ring, heading directly at them, could catch the Super-Constellation in a matter of seconds.

As the ring approached, the pilot saw it emerging as a huge disc, larger than the transport plane. The copilot cried out in fear that the disc would hit them.

At the very last moment, the huge disc seemed to tilt away, its speed greatly reduced as it angled on past the wing. The pilot heaved a sigh of relief as the disc moved away, but his relief was only momentary. The UFO had swung about and was now abreast of the transport, keeping a steady pace at a distance of 100 yards. Now the pilot was able to see a complete and amazing comparison between the UFO and his own craft. At least 30 feet thick at the center, the UFO's diameter was at least three times the Constellation's wing-span. Trembling, the pilot saw a blurred glow along the rim of the UFO, a glow that could have been exhausts, electrical effects, or lights. Certainly, the glow was bright enough to reveal that the disc had a curving surface and that it was three dimensional.

The UFO paced the transport for several moments, then tilted upward, accelerated, and vanished rapidly. Immediately, the pilot radioed the Gander Airport and was told Gander had something on the radar scope, something quite close to the Constellation.

Upon landing, the pilot was given a thorough interrogation, but none of his own questions were answered. At every turn, he was put off by the investigating team. The pilot, who had not previously thought anything about UFOs, asked what the explanation could be if the Air Force denied that UFOs were real. Sorry, no comment.

Absolutely nothing until five days later, when the pilot had a phone call from a top-level government agency scientist who requested an immediate audience. The pilot complied and was shown a series of photos. He was asked to choose the one that most closely matched his own experience. On the third photograph, the pilot felt considerably better. This was not merely a close match of the craft he saw, this was exactly the type of craft that had nearly rammed him, then paced him.

Elated, the pilot made his identification and began asking questions. What were the other sightings like? What kind of craft was this? On and on, in an excited chatter. The scientist took up the photos and put them in his case. Sorry, no comment.

Then the scientist left. And Major Keyhoe entered, irate that any possible conclusions might have been withheld, eager for details. But even the feisty major could not pry for further details. The matter closed here, maddeningly and inconclusive.

Keyhoe has not been one to romanticize the UFOs as many friends have, nor has he been one to withhold some of his most discouraging conclusions, such as the one he reached in relationship to a series of mysterious and unsolved disappearances of Air Force planes in the Pacific.

According to Keyhoe, the Air Force claimed these missing plane reports were actual *disappearances,* a fact the major reported with appropriate exclamation points. To this matter, he added his own mounting suspicion that the missing aircraft had been hit, either intentionally or unintentionally, by UFOs. Even if this were absolutely demonstrable, Keyhoe's statement was not going to go unnoticed. It didn't. And one of the more fascinating parts of taking on the UFO study is that of watching the peppery major and wondering what he is going to say, what he's going to attempt to prove next.

Another staunch believer in the extraterrestrial origin of UFOs is Frank Edwards, who might well be called the Charles Fort of the 1960's. A veteran news commentator and gatherer, Edwards has built up a lively following of listeners and readers who thrive on the unusual, the normally passed over, the downright unexplainable. His specialty is reporting such incidents as the one which took place on the night of April 18, 1962, when a UFO reportedly landed near an electrical substation at Eureka, Utah.

The story Edwards dug up was this: An Air Force spokesman at nearby Stead Air Force Base admitted that the UFO had landed, that the Eureka power station had been out of commission for forty-two minutes, the exact duration of the UFO's period of remaining down. Edwards also found out that the presence of the UFO on the ground had not been admitted to newsmen until it had left and the power delivery resumed.

And in much the same way Dr. Menzel likes to use apparently simple obvious approaches to make his points, so does Frank Edwards. For example: In August of 1965, through virtually the entire central swath of the United States, roughly from North Dakota to Mexico, thousands of persons reported that they saw formations of hovering, maneuvering, streaking, lighted objects in the night sky. Several newspapers gave local reports and accountings of witnesses who had stopped their cars by the side of the road to watch the mysterious formations.

Surely one of the larger sightings of UFOs on recent record. But not so, the Air Force said. The witnesses all saw something, but the objects were definitely identifiable as four stars in the constellation of Orion. Frank Edwards gives the Air Force a certain measure of scorn by relating the fact from two astronomers that at the time of this sighting, the stars in Orion were on the other side of the world.

So much for the Air Force answer that time, but not so much for the Air Force. Edwards says he has no ax to grind with them and seems to come closer than Major Keyhoe to seeing the Air Force in their tiger-by-the-tail position.

Going on the assumption that people do not care to be deceived, Frank Edwards has used his mellow voice, his dramatic delivery, and an insistent rhetoric to hammer home his point: flying saucers are here to stay. The year 1966, according to Edwards, has been one of the best press years in history, and not merely from the point of the number of inches devoted to the subject. He is firmly convinced that many newspapers and publications have gradually come around in their thinking and have abandoned forever the quaint, patronizing tone taken so often with the first batch of saucer sightings in the late 1940's. The venerable newscaster also feels that more people have seen UFOs than ever before, that the number of unsolved cases is on the increase, and that the conclusions are becoming more and more apparent.

Convinced that United States and Russian satellites and space probes are the sources of great interest for our interplanetary visitors, Edwards alleges that there are more instances involving our space program and UFO contacts than the public is aware of. But unlike Major Keyhoe, Edwards seems much more inclined to reason out the purposes of UFOs as friendly and beneficial.

Consulting Edwards for any length of time, one gets the impression that, lurking below the newsman's urgent love for piecing together facts to come up with a story, there is a boyish enthusiasm that has not been dulled by cynicism after having sponsors drop his controversial reportage of the unusual. And one quickly gets the idea that Frank Edwards is literally on pins and needles, waiting for the first major contact. A prolific source of written material on UFOs, Edwards has occasionally been taken to task by the more conservative scientists and laymen for the dynamic force of his conclusions. But this force has gone a long way toward changing the minds of skeptics and preparing disbelievers for the potential of the miraculous which might come. And in this very uncertain subject, one thing is very definite: Frank Edwards cannot be faulted for trying.

Edward J. Ruppelt, the former head of the Air Force Project Bluebook, while not as dynamic as Keyhoe or Edwards, may turn out to be one of the truly great friends of UFOs. Author of one of the more quietly intelligent reports on the subject, Ruppelt has gone to great lengths to explode spurious UFO stories, but he has gone to equally extensive lengths to blast the person—scientist, layman, or military—who says of this phenomenon, "It just can't be." He is one of the few who have set heads spinning by asking some very basic questions. "What constitutes proof?" Ruppelt wants to know. "Does a UFO have to land at the River Entrance to the Pentagon, near the Joint Chiefs of Staff offices? Is it proof when a jet pilot fires at a UFO and sticks to his story even under the threat of court-martial?"

Ruppelt has been instrumental in attempting to achieve a uniform standard of interrogation procedures on UFO sightings, and he has ruthlessly thrown aside such reports as people make when they only think they have seen a strange object. During Ruppelt's tour of duty, he fought the Air Force tendency to throw out all sightings with explanations, and when there were several sightings of the same UFO, or when the observer seemed to see the object at particularly close range, or is uniquely qualified to express an opinion, or simply cannot be shaken in his beliefs, Ruppelt fought for carefully classifying the data.

One example of Ruppelt's approach came when two Air Force colonels made detailed sightings of UFOs over the Carson sink area outside Reno, Nev. The reports were detailed, the colonels were quite positive of what they saw, and they steadfastly withstood all intelligence attempts to shake their stories. Nevertheless, the official conclusion reached was that the two men had probably witnessed some flight of experimental aircraft, probably the Navy batwings.

When Ruppelt got hold of the case, he began checking records and quickly discovered that each of the colonels had a rather strong reason for insisting what he saw was real. The

Pentagon later confirmed the fact that the colonels were both in a position to know about every aircraft from every branch of the service. That knowledge included current experimental and prototype models as well.

This made the colonels even more reliable as witnesses, and although it did not offer proof positive that the UFOs were interplanetary, it did qualify them for the unsolved file, a fact that gives Ruppelt the stature of an attorney who has taken on a difficult case and brought back a hung jury. His point of view is that there is danger in assuming UFOs can't possibly be real, a point of view that many saucer fans look upon as bending over backwards to be fair.

Although Ruppelt's monumental study, *The Report on Unidentified Flying Objects* was written in 1956, it is dated only in the sense that it does not include data on the later sightings. But as a work of good reporting and objectivity, it is a must for any serious student of UFO lore, and is particularly recommended as an excellent middle-of-the-road compromise between Major Keyhoe on one side and Dr. Menzel on the other. It is Ruppelt's final conclusion that, somewhere along the way, the earth satellite program will begin providing some more conclusive answers.

Two times before Ruppelt's report appeared, "official" word was released that UFO reports had been solved to the satisfaction of investigating agencies. And promptly after each such case, the number of sightings and unsolved cases began to take a sharp jump. In Edward Ruppelt's conclusion that there is a healthy number of unsolved cases, there is a good balance of weight for the argument that UFOs are more than three-dimensional objects for which there is no explanation.

John G. Fuller is probably better known among UFO fans as the author of *Incident at Exeter*, a serious probe of the

September 3, 1965, sightings near Exeter, N.H. As detailed and well-compiled as a book of this sort can be, Fuller's work does everything but offer actual proof that UFOs are really interplanetary vehicles. Certainly, Fuller does offer a kind of proof that is fairly unique among UFO books. Not only does he include reports of people who claim to have seen mysterious objects, he also offers as evidence the fact that he, too, has seen them. And the unshakable belief in this sighting certainly falls in among some of the probing questions asked by Ruppelt.

A columnist for the *Saturday Review,* Fuller has put something in the pot by staking his reputation on his own report and on his book. The probing questions he asks and the intelligent conclusions he makes may have been one of the deciding factors in causing the Air Force to inaugurate their study in conjunction with the University of Colorado. Fuller has built an argument for an immediate and full-scale investigation plus the all-important fact of disclosure of these facts to the interested public. This is a case of a man going to bat for something he wanted.

Not all UFO believers are so successful, and in fact, some find themselves in the position of being reluctant believers. They know their senses have told them something was there, something out of the ordinary. But what their senses could not tell them was the sometimes ironic, often irrevocable events which would follow.

Such a person is Dale Spaur. In April of 1966, Dale Spaur was a deputy for the Sheriff of Portage County, Ohio. On duty with another deputy, Barney Neff, Spaur spotted a red-and-white 1959 Ford alongside the road between Randolph and Atwater, Ohio, and with that incident, an irrevocable series of events were unleashed.

Checking out the parked car, Spaur and Neff found it filled with walkie-talkies and other radios. On the side of the car, a strange emblem was painted. As he noticed it, Spaur also heard a humming sound behind him.

Turning, he saw a huge saucer-shaped craft rising from the woods. The entire underside of this large object emitted an intense, purplish-white light. Spaur felt paralyzed for a moment, then realized he had the sudden impression that he should not touch the car with the strange emblem painted on it. If he did, Spaur believed, the car would disappear.

Both Spaur and Neff dashed for their cruiser and radioed in to the headquarters they serve. At headquarters, other calls had come in describing the UFO. Spaur was ordered to "Shoot it." Once more, Spaur felt the strange compulsion that he could not perform, that he certainly could not shoot at the hovering UFO, which he estimated to be perhaps 20 feet high and 50 feet across.

The order came in over the radio. "Follow it." And Dale Spaur did. He estimates he hit speeds of more than 100 miles an hour as he raced eastward through Ohio and into Pennsylvania, chasing after the craft. The UFO almost seemed to be playing a game, encouraging the chase, waiting at intersections, doubling back, hovering nearby. When the cruiser ran out of gas, the chase ended and the disc disappeared, but in some ways, the story had only begun.

The subject of local interest because of the sighting, Spaur was questioned and interviewed by Air Force investigators, newsmen, and magazine writers. He seemed different. Perhaps it was fear, perhaps it was something that happens to men when they see something completely outside any frame of reference they have ever had. But Spaur began to feel moody.

"I don't know what it was," his wife said. "He came home that day and I never saw him more frightened before. He acted strange, listless. He just sat around. He was very pale. Then later he got real nervous, and he started to run away. He'd just disappear for days and days. I wouldn't see him."

After one of these disappearances, Spaur came home late, not sure what had got into him. He felt confused, frightened. He grabbed his wife and shook her, hard. He kept right on shaking, leaving big, ugly bruises on her arm. He still is not sure why. But he does know that his strange behavior cost him his wife. Shortly after the shaking incident, Daneise Spaur filed assault and battery charges against her husband, and was awarded a divorce and custody of their two children.

Dale Spaur saw the flying saucer once again. Knowing the police radio band was monitored by civilians, the sheriff's department gave the UFO a code name, Floyd, taken from Spaur's middle name.

Alone in his cruiser, Spaur was given the night watch. As he drove east on Interstate Highway 80-S, he looked up from his lonely vigil and saw the UFO. He flicked on the radio and whispered into it, "Floyd's with me." Spaur was alone this time. He did nothing about the UFO. He smoked a cigaret and stared straight ahead for nearly fifteen minutes. Then the UFO disappeared and Spaur has not seen it since. Shortly after this, Spaur lost his job.

A quiet, taciturn man, it is difficult for us to know what Dale Spaur thinks in his new life. No longer a deputy sheriff, he walks to work each day, lives in a cheap hotel, and barely has enough money to give himself meager meals and pay the court-ordered child support. He is one of the growing legion who can offer no other rational explanation for UFOs other than the fact that he knows they are real—he has seen one.

And he wishes he never had. Most of the others connected with Dale Spaur's saucer have either recanted or refuse to mention it.

One UFO investigator, Mrs. Coral Lorenzen, combines the traits of attractiveness, an avid interest in her subject, a sharp eye for public relations, and a determination that there will be no nonsense in higher echelons of official research organizations. She is the founder of APRO, the Aerial Phenomena Research Organization, which holds forth at 3910 Kleindale Road, Tucson, Ariz., and puts forth a fiery publication giving accounts of recent sightings. Always on the lookout for a new person to convert to belief in UFOs, Mrs. Lorenzen wastes no time in enlisting whatever news media she can to publicize the more dramatic sightings.

A former employee for an Air Force officer at the Holloman Air Force Base, she became enraged at the apparent doctrine of writing off all sightings as being explainable by means of natural events. Mrs. Lorenzen is not only convinced of the interplanetary nature of UFOs, she has claimed to have had in her possession chunks of material from an unmanned disc which exploded in mid-air. According to Dr. Menzel, she was not very anxious to give these fragments to the Air Force for analysis, but Mrs. Lorenzen did want a representative of her organization to be present during the analysis.

As a part of her earnest belief that contact between some segment of mankind and the UFOs is imminent, Mrs. Lorenzen has released a fascinating story, supposedly passed on to her by confidantes and secret news sources at the Holloman Air Force Base. Writing in *Fate* Magazine, Mrs. Lorenzen tells of a sighting which took place near the Holloman Base. The UFOs performed a set of precise maneuvers before disappearing. A visual confirmation was made by a trained radar operator who described the UFOs as brown and football shaped.

"Probably the most disturbing information relating to this sighting," Mrs. Lorenzen said, "was that one or both of the objects was responding alternately with the standard FAA (Federal Aeronautics Administration) recognition signal (sometimes called IFF).

"To avoid the necessity of having to depend entirely on radar 'skin track,' i.e., reflection of radar beam from the plane's surface, there is in use in most military and commercial aircraft an interrogate signal . . . transmitted periodically from the tracking ground station. This signal consists of a series of pulses arranged in a particular time sequence or 'code.' When the . . . combination receiver and transmitter receives the correct code, it responds by transmitting a code of its own which is received at the ground station. This is called a 'recognition signal.' . . . It was one of these codes that the two football-shaped objects were beaming alternately while in flight . . ."

If, as some of her critics seem to suggest, Mrs. Lorenzen is overly dramatic at times, she certainly has the ability to come up with an intriguing case history when it most counts.

Another important fan of UFO beliefs is Alfred Chop, former civilian director of publicity for the Air Force and an important secondary hero to Major Keyhoe in Keyhoe's book *Flying Saucers from Outer Space*.

Limited by the security requirements of his Air Force job before he left it, Chop emerges as being sympathetic to Keyhoe and interested in providing all the help he can. Following the precedent of becoming more convinced by a close association with the abundant UFO data, Chop has been in the rare position of seeing official Air Force point of view see-saw over a period of years. He has also seen how easy it is to discredit some sightings while others must remain as solid potentialities. Perhaps it was the sheer bulk of "good" sightings or the smaller but nevertheless significant number of sightings which were unimpeachable that won Chop over. Whatever the reason, he is now on record as being convinced that UFOs are of alien origin.

Gerald Heard, the noted author and lecturer, brings a touch of literary respectability and mystical stature to UFO fans with his study, *Is Another World Watching?* Somewhat dated so far as incidents and case histories are concerned, Heard's book still stands up seventeen years after publication in this country because of its carefully built argument that we are, indeed, being watched by an alien race from Mars. Mr. Heard finds this alien group quite likely to offer us friendship and a new way of life.

Usually more of a philosophical or scholarly worker, dealing with the abstract or the abstruse, Mr. Heard has brought an unusual clarity of style and approach to this study. Beyond asking us to accept UFO theory, Heard seems quite concerned with our future as a race, as a people, as a civilization. "There seems then, here and now," he says, "no right feeling (any more than right and adequate reason) why we should refuse, with either heart or mind, the present possibility that hangs over us. It may be an offer . . . Why should we refuse at least to consider it?"

Another distinguished literary believer in the reality of UFOs is Pulitzer Prize winner MacKinlay Kantor who had believed that unidentified flying objects exist for some years. Working with retired Air Force General Curtis Le May on a book, *Mission with Le May. My Story,* Kantor heard the former Air Force commander state bluntly: "Repeat again:

There were some cases of UFOs we could not explain. Never could." This added to Kantor's convictions. And then, Mac-Kinlay Kantor saw a UFO.

Writing in *Popular Science*, Kantor tells of his experience on a Florida island, Siesta Key. "It looked like the top third of an apricot . . . Also, there seemed to be some sort of rim around the bottom."

Using the object's relationship between some nearby trees, Kantor was later able to make calculations dealing with the UFO's elevation above the horizon, but he was unable to do anything significant about the size and altitude.

Kantor's UFO "was motionless. It moved neither to right nor left, for a matter of minutes. It did not appear to become any larger; hence it was not advancing. It did not appear to become any smaller; hence it was not receding." Kantor kept the UFO in sight for approximately four minutes before it disappeared. Ever since, he has been looking for others . . . and believing.

New York based philosopher James B. Silverman, director of the Pragmatic Realist Foundation, is willing to go on record as believing most of the well-authenticated sightings are real objects, even though this means some trouble from his own organization. The Pragmatic Realists, Silverman says, are often more hidebound than scientists. They take a wait-and-see-how-it-works attitude to most things and are interested only in observable phenomena. Silverman says, "We can no longer turn our backs on the possibilities afforded by UFOs. Even if they should be proved to be nothing more than globs of light, or reflections from the backs of birds—which I seriously doubt—they will have proved the point that man not only has expectations but that man is working toward making those expectations pay off. I'm willing to stand up and be counted among those who believe something they haven't seen. It was a difficult choice at first, but after I made it, there seemed to be no alternative."

Dr. George R. Wait of the Carnegie Institute of Technology, a leading authority on the ionosphere, was also willing to stand up and be counted. "If the reports of reversals, sharp turns, and descents are fully confirmed," he said, "then no natural phenomena, to my knowledge, would explain such sightings."

These, then, are some of the many staunch believers in the possibilities and potentials associated with UFOs. They are people who have expressed their beliefs at times when to do so might have branded them as unreliable commentators and observers. Some of them have not seen any form of UFO, but accept on faith and conviction what others have seen. Their beliefs were not easily formed, but now they are not easily shaken. Now, as friends of UFOs, they ask you to take precisely the same approach.

CHAPTER NINE

The Contactees

To say that Betty and Barney Hill claim to have been inside a flying saucer and in some form of communication with the beings who operated it is to understate the case. It is more accurate to say that Betty and Barney Hill are quite convinced that they were inside an alien spacecraft, and that an intensive course of hypnosis, administered by a prominent Boston psychiatrist, did not, in any way, shake their stories.

Many things about their stories jibe, leading to some inferences which begin to form a part of a fantastic picture. Among these inferences comes the memory of a map shown to Betty Hill by a person she thought to be the leader of a flying saucer crew. The map was nearly meaningless to Betty, who does not have much of a background in astronomy. But a map of the constellation Pegasus jogged her memory somewhat, and if Betty's memory serves her at all well in this matter, the home base of the UFO on which she and Barney spent time might easily have been Markab, in the Pegasus constellation. The belief of a Russian astronomer that intelligent radio emissions may be coming from that area adds even greater interest to the Hills' story.

In addition to their contentions that they were subjected to apparent physical examinations, complete with the taking of

X-rays and skin specimens, the Hills provide descriptions of their hosts. Notable in these descriptions is the fact that the aliens had weak jaws and much less musculature about the mouth than most earthlings. Also, these beings seemed to communicate by a process involving some form of telepathy. Barney, in particular, seemed to hear instructions and concepts in his head. Both Betty and Barney agree that their hosts had eyes that extended further around the curve of the cheek bones, allowing for a far greater peripheral vision than humans enjoy.

Lastly and of no less importance, the visitors seemed to have the ability—mental or mechanical—to block out memories and plant suggestions which were quite difficult but not impossible to resist. Sounds a bit like Lamont Cranston who, as The Shadow, had "the mysterious power to cloud men's minds." But it is a definite part of the Hills' story and, like all the other elements, there seems no way of disproving or shaking it.

The Hills' description comes a long way from the affable creature with the smoked glasses spotted by Capt. Hooten. But then, so do all the descriptions of persons who claim to have made these fantastic voyages.

George Adamski, one of the most famous of all UFO fans, gave a description of a Venusian male of approximately twenty-six or twenty-seven, with shoulder-length hair and a sort of baggy, skisuit-type uniform. This person was seen by Adamski on a memorable afternoon in 1952, after he had traveled to the California Desert near Parker, Ariz., with friends, following the deep conviction that this was the day he would be contacted.

An amateur astronomer, Adamski had considerable equipment and had been a rich source of sighting claims. He had also produced controversial photographs and, indeed, was to add to the controversy today with photographs, reports of a conversation, and with plaster-of-paris casts of the footprints of his Venusian visitor.

Prior to his November 20th contact, Adamski had made any number of trips to the desert, undoubtedly following information and reports supplied by George Van Tassel, another contactee of some note. Driving through the desert with his friends, Adamski gave directions by intuition, and shortly after noon they saw a two-motored plane, apparently on a conventional flight. Just as this plane disappeared in the distance, Adamski and his friends noticed a huge cigar-shaped ship, seemingly at a drift toward them.

Adamski and his friends watched the ship for a moment, nervously bobbling the opportunity to set up a rented motion picture camera for pictures. One of the party, a doctor and World War II Air Force veteran, noticed an insignia on the side of the craft. Well acquainted with the insignia of foreign and American airplanes, the doctor was unable to make any kind of an identification. (Could it have been the same as the strange insignia seen by patrolman Zamora on the occasion of his UFO sighting near Socorro, N.M.?)

After the cigar craft disappeared, Adamski had the distinct impression that it had been connected with a potential for a personal contact which would involve him. "Don't ask me . . . how I knew . . . I have a habit of following my feelings, and that is the way I felt. But I cannot tell you why." He made arrangements with his friends so that he could be left at some distance from them, but in their sight so that he would have witnesses if his intuition proved correct and he was visited.

He was not alone for more than five minutes before he was able to see the appearance of a small craft as it settled down through a saddle between the peaks of two mountains. The saucer chose a strategic location. "It did not lower itself entirely below the crest of the mountain," Adamski said. "Only the lower portion settled below the crest, while the upper, or dome section, remained above the crest and in full sight of the rest of my party who were back there watching. Yet it was in such a position that I could see the entire ship as it hovered in the cove ahead of me. At the same time, many miles of the highway and surrounding terrain were in full view of the crew within the saucer."

Adamski took a series of photos of the craft, then noticed a man standing approximately a quarter of a mile away. The man motioned Adamski to approach. Cautiously, he moved forward, noting that the man was about 5½ feet tall and weighing an estimated 135 pounds. He wore clothing that looked similar to a skiing uniform and his long, shoulder-length hair was blowing in the wind.

Adamski says the man's face was round, given to an extremely high forehead. His eyes were large, grey-green in color, and slightly aslant at the outer corners. The cheek bones were higher than those of an Occidental, but not so high as an Indian or an Oriental. There was apparently little or no hair on the man's face and his skin coloring resembled a medium suntan.

Realizing that this man was related to the saucer, Adamski began attempts at communication and was forced to use sign language and diagrams in the sand. By these means, he established that they were on earth, third planet from the sun. Now what was the origin of the UFO? By holding up two fingers, the man conveyed to Adamski that his home base had been Venus, a word he repeated after Adamski uttered it first.

In answer to such questions as "Why are you coming to

earth?" Adamski was given the answer that the intentions were friendly and that the visitors were concerned with radiations coming from earth.

As questions popped into Adamski's mind, he asked them and was given answers:

Were our atomic explosion experiments affecting outer space?

Definitely.

Had the previous atomic experiments resulted in any form of a cumulative build-up?

Yes.

Had the visitor come directly from Venus in his small craft?

No. The smaller craft had been transported by the larger, cigar-shaped craft Adamski had seen earlier.

Then Adamski discovered that he could convey questions to the visitor by thinking of visual images. He received an affirmative nod when he pictured the cigar-shaped craft acting as a sort of space-going aircraft carrier. More mental communications revealed that the UFOs were powered by magnetic-controlled force fields and that the smaller discs—the ones often referred to as foo planes—were not piloted. They were, in effect, the eyes of the scout ships and cigar craft, and they sent back reports of observations. Often, explosions seen in space were these tiny scouting discs which had developed a short circuit or crosscurrent problem.

Adamski was also led to believe that space travel was quite common and that there were communications made between several planets and between several different systems. There had already been scores of landings on earth and there would undoubtedly be more.

Had there been any deaths involved in space travel to earth?

Yes. Flying saucers and other spacecraft were mechanical objects and subject to failure. This had happened before and lives had been lost.

Why haven't there been more public-type landings?

Because the space people fear the reactions of many of the people living on earth.

Had other earthlings been taken into spacecraft?

The answer was a guarded yes, causing a question to persist in Adamski's mind. He speaks of pushing the point in the matter of a particular case and is given an answer, but warned not to discuss it further. The individual case in Adamski's mind may have been George Van Tassel, whom we will meet, or more probably Dr. Daniel Fry, who, on the night of July 4, 1950, claims to have been transported in a cargo carrier from New Mexico to New York and back again within the time span of about half an hour. We will also meet Daniel Fry in some detail.

How many other planets are populated?

Nearly all.

After a few more questions, it became time for the visitor to leave. Very pointedly, the visitor made three distinct sets of footmarkings with the embossed soles of his shoes. Then he motioned to Adamski to follow him and the two approached the small craft, hovering in the wind. Another figure was visible moving within the ship. At close quarters, Adamski was able to get an idea of why UFOs seemed so elusive to the eyes and to the camera. The ship had a definite furry, translucent glow. As it hovered, three balls of the landing gear seemed to descend in entire agreement with Adamski's controversial photograph. The sun, reflecting on the surface of the ship, caused prismatic rays of light to bounce from it.

"I noticed a round ball at the very top that looked like a

heavy lens of some kind. And it glowed. I wondered if this could be used as one end of a magnetic pole to draw their power from space as they were moving through it."

Perhaps Adamski moved too close to the ship. His right shoulder came under the outer edge of a protruding flange and he was jostled severely by a force he could not see. It took three months for the soreness and pain to disappear.

After being politely refused admission into the craft, Adamski was asked for a favor. His Venusian visitor would like one of the photographic film plates Adamski had exposed earlier. A polite farewell was exchanged, the visitor promised to return Adamski's film, and then he stepped into the craft, which moved off into the sky.

When it was gone, Adamski's friends moved in closer and made plaster-of-paris casts of the footprints. One of the party photographed them, but the results were indeterminate. Another member of the party made careful sketches of the prints, which seem to resemble a combination of American Indian symbols and ancient hieroglyphics. To date, neither Adamski nor anyone else has been able to get anything significant in the way of a meaning from these prints, each of which was different.

On the morning of December 13, 1952, Adamski's Venusian friend returned in what was almost a routine event, if such a thing can be said of any flying saucer incident. While making photos of a saucer through his telescope, Adamski had the feeling that it would be bringing his friend with the photograph that had been taken from him earlier. The saucer approached to within 100 feet of him and one of the portholes was opened. A hand appeared in the porthole, waved, then dropped the photographic plate. The hand waved again, and then the craft moved off into the skies.

After retrieving the plate, Adamski took it to his friend, another photographer, for corroboration in the developing procedure. When the developing and finishing were completed, the results were slightly more than bargained for. In addition to the photograph of the saucer which had been taken back on November 20th, there was another photograph, described by Adamski as strange and having accompanying markings which neither he nor the scientists to whom he claims he gave the photograph could decipher.

With Adamski's recent death, several booklets and pamphlets have been rushed into print, some of which contain more of his photographs of UFOs, others of which reportedly contain evidence of his secret confidences with the space people. In some ways, it seems unfortunate that Adamski's death by natural causes has been attributed by some amateur UFO groups to "a broken heart" because the scientists failed to give him recognition for his devotion and dedication to the principle that UFOs are real. Such incidents have made it more difficult for the newcomer to approach the subjects of Mr. Adamski and UFOs with objectivity.

George Adamski has left behind him a tremendous bulk of work in writing and in photograph on the UFO phenomenon, on the possibilities of life—intelligent life—from other systems, assurances of the peaceful intentions of our visitors, and a great deal of controversy, loose ends, and speculation.

Giant Rock, a small landing field carved out of the California Desert near Yucca Valley, is the reported scene of many UFO landings, contacts, and messages. The tremendous surge of activity here was begun when Van Tassel was contacted by persons operating saucerlike spacecraft. They asked Van Tassel to come with them, inspect their spacecraft, and travel inside it. Since that time, Van Tassel says it has been made clear to him that his Giant Rock home is a "Natural cone of receptivity" making it quite sensitive for telepathic communications. He was also told that he might consider devoting his time to the study of UFOs, to the ways of the space people, and to the ways in which he could help earth people. As a result, thousands of people have thronged to Giant Rock in hopes of learning more from Van Tassel about the UFOs and the people behind them.

Van Tassel's book, *I Rode a Flying Saucer,* while no great literary shakes, earned its keep for the publisher and for the author. But it was Van Tassel's newsletter, sent on subscription, that began to pay off for him. When you have a subscription list, you can send out literature for small booklets, and when you have virtually a hot line to the source of information, there is no end to the number of small booklets which may be produced. Visitors to Giant Rock came away impressed and armed with information. Study groups were formed, and soon Giant Rock became a Mecca toward which thousands of sincere UFO fans made a pilgrimage. Conventions were held and information was exchanged. Thousands of people held discussions during the day and watched the skies at night, avid of sighting a flying saucer.

Van Tassel found that he was capable of "receiving" telepathic messages in much the same way a medium acts as the go-between for the spiritual and corporeal world. Without actually entering the trance state, Van Tassel was able to develop a working relationship with some of the space people who were, more or less, assigned to public relations tasks with earth people.

One of the messages Van Tassel received was: "Salutations. My identity is Quel, 72nd projection, 15th wave, realms of Schare [a saucer station in space]. We are passing over your cone of receptivity, 172,000 miles above you. Our center requests that I inform you. You will see more of us if you watch the skies." Van Tassel did watch the skies, and from this vigil came photographs, more messages, some predictions of events to come, and some explanations of events that had taken place.

It was only natural that Van Tassel become an object of scorn and curiosity because of the publicity. He was variously suspect of having established a numbered Swiss banking account into which he poured thousands of dollars of profit, of being deluded, of being a paranoid schizophrenic, of being a humble, saintly man, of being a modern P. T. Barnum. Then again, another report belies this by telling of his being hospitalized for malnutrition, but not because his choice of food was so poor, rather because he couldn't afford better nourishment.

On frequent occasions, Van Tassel was contacted by saucers that landed on earth and took him for rides. Possibly aware of scorn with which he was regarded, Van Tassel said he really did not care. The important thing to him was the fact that he had seen with his own eyes and that was sufficient. George Van Tassel, Giant Rock, and the natural cone of receptivity remain as one of the more controversial aspects of UFO reports, even so far as the most devoted fans are concerned.

Truman Bethurum of Prescott, Ariz., became another of the famed contactees on the morning of July 28, 1952. A construction worker by trade, Bethurum claims he was in the Nevada desert, looking for seashells which would be the result of an ancient ocean intrusion. At a time shortly before dawn, he saw a flying saucer and was introduced to its friendly crew. The leader was an unusually handsome woman who made such an impact on Bethurum that he was momentarily unable to speak. He describes this attractive woman as, amazingly enough, the grandmother of two, "a queen among women," wearing a bright red skirt, a short-sleeved black velvet blouse, and a black beret with a red piping.

The implication given by Bethurum in his book *Aboard a Flying Saucer* and by other UFO believers who discussed his subsequent experiences with him is that he was chosen for friendship and contact because of his great humility, his lack of skepticism, and because he was not very bright.

During a friendship which lasted for several months, Truman Bethurum was contacted several times, discussing things of a philosophical nature and showing a growing concern for the way life was developing here on earth. At the attractive grandmother's invitation, Bethurum accompanied her and her crew back to the flying saucer's home base, described as a planet called Clarion, which has not yet been sighted by astronomers from earth because of that planet's location directly behind the moon and because of that planet's parallel orbit with the moon.

There are many schools in the United States and scattered throughout the world where an individual may earn a diploma without ever having set foot on the campus. In fact, anything more than a cursory visit to the campus would probably be discouraged. Some of these correspondence-course schools are highly reputable and, indeed, many noted universities throughout the world join in mail-order education provisions, and degrees granted by them are among the most respected. But there are diploma mills, granting bachelor's degrees, conferring master of arts or sciences degrees, and bestowing the lofty title of Ph.D., which is sufficient for the nominee to call himself doctor.

Dr. Daniel Fry is not such a doctor, he is a graduate of St. Andrews College of London, has been involved with numerous missile and space programs, and was a consultant for the noted California Institute of Technology. While employed by the Aerojet General Corporation at the White Sands Proving Grounds near Las Cruces, N.M., Dr. Fry reported an experience which he could just as easily have forgotten or passed along quietly. Had he done so, he would certainly have run less of a risk of being looked down upon by many other scientists and being considered a possible fraud by yet others.

On the night of July 4, 1950, Daniel Fry not only claimed to have seen a flying saucer, he "touched it, entered it, and even made a short test hop as a passenger. Also, I have communicated at some length with its operator."

Missing a company car and bus that would have taken him from the White Sands Testing Grounds into nearby Las Cruces for a Fourth of July celebration, Fry felt resigned to staying in his room and reading, but the heat of the evening was unbearable and he decided on a walk out into the desert.

His first inkling of anything unusual was when a star in the sky seemed to "go out." But it was no star, Dr. Fry says, it was an oblate spheroid about 30 feet in diameter. It settled slowly to the ground at a distance of about 70 feet from him after approaching at rather slow speeds.

An associate designer on many Air Force projects, Fry approached the UFO with amazement that an object of such design could fly at all. The realization that this was, indeed, a close-up sighting began to weigh on him. Who would substantiate his story? Who would believe him? "I had read of the ridicule heaped upon those who had stated they had seen unexplained objects flying in the air," he said. "How much worse would I be criticized if I claimed to have seen one land

and been close enough to touch it, yet had no proof of the fact except a flattened patch of bush [that broke when the UFO touched down]."

That was only the beginning of Fry's troubles. As he ran his hand over the surface of the craft, a voice seemed to come out of the air at his side. Even more so than his descriptions that were to follow, the opening gambit of conversation with his alien visitor brought the rooftop down on Dan Fry.

"Better not touch that hull, pal, it's still hot!" came the voice. And after Fry backed off, momentarily bewildered, the voice spoke again. "Take it easy, pal, you're among friends."

The warning and follow-up were loud enough to give Fry a start, and irritate him. He snapped back angrily and was told that he stood the danger of killing himself by touching the hull of the object, which was still slightly active. The field about the object, he was told, repels all matter, and was described to him as the anti aspect of the binding energy of the atom. After more conversation, Fry was told that he had been chosen for contact because of his scientific background and his open mind.

The visitor went on at length to tell Fry how so many scientists think that because they know all the available information about a subject that there is no more information to learn. He was given a brief lecture on the importance of returning to all the knowledge we have accumulated and following through with it or, as the voice told Fry, "go back down the limb on which you are trapped to the point where it joins the main trunk and then start up again."

After a time, Fry was invited to board and ride the spacecraft. After a portal opened for him, Fry stepped into a compartment he described as being about 9 feet deep and 7 feet wide, with a ceiling at a height of nearly 6 feet. He discovered four seats and an object that resembled a motion picture camera. A light issued from the lens. Sitting in one of the chairs, he was asked where he would like to go. The suggestion was made that he might enjoy seeing one of the favorite sights of interstellar astronauts, the light pattern of New York City from an altitude of 20 miles. The trip to New York and back would take about half an hour, just as much time as Fry's host had to spare at the moment.

The astounded Fry agreed, realizing he would be traveling at speeds of 8,000 miles an hour. He was told that the projectorlike device was a viewing screen through which he would be able to see the terrain below him as the object moved. Watching in stunned amazement, Fry saw the lights of Las Cruces, the highway from Las Cruces to El Paso, Tex., and finally the city lights of El Paso, the snake-like curve of the Rio Grande River, and then the surface of the earth, miles below. At this point, he was told the craft was raising itself into the sky at a rate of ½ mile per second.

Details of the flight were explained along with the reason why high-speed acceleration in spacecraft is possible, "The force which accelerates the vehicle is identical in nature to a gravitational field. It not only acts upon every atom of the vehicle itself but also acts equally upon every atom of mass which is within it, including the pilot or passengers . . . Our only limit of acceleration is the limit of available force."

When Fry asked for a description of the principles on which flying saucers work, he was told that he would have to be given an entirely new concept of the laws of physics, that our current use of the laws provide for only a 30 per cent efficiency because they are much too complex. "Your greatest need is to discover the utter simplicity of the basic laws or facts of nature. Then you will be able to produce effects which now seem to you to be impossible."

As the saucer neared New York City, Fry's host introduced himself as A-lan, a direct descendant of the peoples of Lemuria, a continent located in the Pacific and sometimes referred to as Mu. A-lan told Fry of another continent in the midst of the Atlantic Ocean, Atlantis. At first, the two continents engaged in a friendly rivalry in the matter of scientific developments, but as time passed, the competition was no longer friendly, and the result was the sort of war that would make an atomic war appear puny in comparison. The resulting holocaust caused a major upheaval in the earth's physical configuration, and the radiation wiped out mankind. But A-lan did not have time to finish his story. The craft had already passed over New York City, shown Fry a remarkable view of the shimmering lights 20 miles below, then streaked back across the continent to New Mexico.

Fry was told that landings were possible but that it was difficult for the aliens to leave their ships for any length of time unless they had taken long, careful steps to work up to a tolerance for the atmospheric and bacterial content of earth. A-lan's final words were, "So long, Dan. Step out and take care of yourself until we return."

Fry's work at White Sands was soon completed and he returned to California. But his experience weighed heavily on him, and on two occasions he drove 800 miles up to his retreat in Southern Oregon. On both occasions, he was contacted by A-lan, who seemed motivated by urgency. A-lan asked Fry to write a book and make public his contact and what he had learned. Fry reminded A-lan of the scorn and ridicule the skeptics would heap upon him and A-lan reminded Fry that virtually no worthwhile person or idea had not, at some time, met with great opposition. He went on at great length to discuss the need for following natural laws and for escaping from the competitiveness that can lead only to war and extinction.

Fry published his account and as much of A-lan's advice as he could accurately remember. And Fry was certainly met with scorn, ridicule, and accusations of perpetrating a hoax to insure income from a profitable lecture and writing career. The more official UFO reports tend to slough off Fry's experiences as being highly unsubstantiated and subject to question. Dr. Menzel reserves a few acerbic paragraphs for Dan Fry in his report, and there the matter rests. But Dan Fry is not content. Now a member of the National Investigating Committee on Aerial Phenomena, he uses every possible opportunity to tell what he knows and pass along the message to any who will listen.

Howard Menger of Highbridge, N.J., is another who claims to have traveled in a flying saucer to other worlds. While walking in the woods near his home one evening, Menger was approached by long-haired aliens who wore highly luminous beltbuckles and invited him for a ride in which he saw the planet Venus at close hand. Menger reported seeing winding streams, domed houses, and exceptionally beautiful people. He also told of a visit to the moon, which is, indeed, inhabited, and from which he brought back a lunar potato, which he allegedly handed over to government scientists who have refused to make their findings public.

George Adamski.

George W. Van Tassel.

Truman Bethurum.

Daniel Fry.

Howard Menger.

Five men who have ridden in UFOs . . . or so they say.

Five men with varying backgrounds and different stories, but only the beginning of the contactees.

CHAPTER TEN

UFO Study Groups

Loren Eiseley, a noted naturalist, has said, "In a universe whose size is beyond human imagining, where our world floats like a dust more in the void of night, men have grown inconceivably lonely. We scan the time scale and the mechanisms of life itself for portents and signs of the invisible . . . We watch the stars but the signs are uncertain . . . Lights come and go in the night sky. Men, troubled at last by the things they build, may toss in their sleep and dream bad dreams, or lie awake while the meteors whisper greenly overhead."

Perhaps it is loneliness, perhaps it is some form of guilt, perhaps it is curiosity that causes the fourteen people to be assembled in the dimly lit living room of a small, two-bedroom home in Lynwood, a southeastern suburb of Los Angeles, Calif. The host and hostess are barely in their thirties and have two young daughters, both sound asleep. In the same room with them is the sleeping child of a visiting couple. The host holds a position of responsibility with the telephone company. One of his guests is a publicist for a motion picture production company. Another is a husband-and-wife team, an interior decorator and insurance company executive, respectively. Also in the group is the mother-in-law of the host, another young couple who have driven nearly 25 miles for the evening, and yet another couple, both of whom are aircraft workers.

Scattered about the room are children's toys, magazines of a general interest, and several books about flying saucers. A stack of newsletters from George Van Tassel are on the coffee table along with a stack of carbon copies of the "minutes" of a meeting that was held in this same room a week before.

A few of the guests help themselves to coffee and the mother-in-law of the host stirs uncomfortably in her seat. "They're here," she says. "I can feel them. I think they're restless." Suddenly, the host closes his eyes and begins to speak. "Good evening," he says. "We have a great deal to accomplish tonight and I want to get down to business."

Side conversations halt. Most of the persons settle into their chairs or sofas and lean their heads back. A few others watch the host intently as he continues. "I am pleased to see so many of you here tonight."

The telephone begins to ring and the hostess gets up and leaves the room to answer it. Her husband goes on in a manner that is much more forthright than his normal, rather shy manner of speech. "Your group has become too large and you must split up to form new groups. I think it best that you all meet together not more than once a month. Of course, we have no objection to you meeting socially. We are pleased that you have become friends because of us. But tonight, we are going to choose a speaker who will talk for another group. The new speaker will pick up the thread of the transmission *now* . . ."

A long pause as the persons in the room look about, exchanging glances. One young man begins to squirm in his seat and stretches his long legs.

"Without breaking continuity." the host suddenly shouts, his face contorted through effort. He opens his eyes and looks at the long-legged young man. "They meant you. Didn't you feel it?"

"I don't know," the young man said. "But I can swear those exact words—without breaking continuity—popped into my mind. I knew you were going to say that. I guess it was a coincidence."

"Coincidence, nothing," the host's mother-in-law says. "They want you to continue. Close your eyes and relax for a moment, then try it."

The hostess returns to the room and mentions the name of the wife of a dentist. "She can't make it tonight, and she wonders if some of you who live closer to her could stop over at her place next Friday."

The host smiles at the young man. "There's your new group. You'll be the spokesman. Now, let's get them back in and see what they've got to say."

After a long silence, the host speaks up again. "They don't want me to do it . . ." he points at the young man, ". . . they want you to continue."

"I'll try," the young man says, and he does, but finally, he is forced to admit failure. "It's too confusing. I'm not sure what's me and what's them."

"Relax," the mother-in-law says, "and just let it come. I'll tell you what. I'll try to get something and when it starts, you see if you can follow it, word for word in your own mind. But relax."

The young man nods agreement and a few moments later, the mother-in-law begins speaking. "We are very near your sector tonight, our smaller craft are out charting magnetic-force fields and atmospheric disturbances. I have been asked to convey to you our concern that you seem to place so much emphasis on seeing us before you believe us. Our business is too important for parlor tricks and miracles. You all have abilities and powers which you should develop. You should all be able to communicate the way we do with you, and I urge you to experiment when you are at a distance from one another. You must investigate the natural abilities you possess and develop them as you would develop any technique you value. For the next few minutes, we will transmit pictures to you, and then I will describe what we have sent, after you have had a chance to compare your own impressions. Then we must work together on developing the confidence of your new spokesman."

For the next half hour, the group concentrates on the images supposedly being beamed to them. The newly designated spokesman bravely speaks up first with his impressions and is told by the host that his impressions are correct.

The new spokesman finally admits he has the urge to say something: "Do not expect all groups to be alike. The personalities will vary according to the people in the groups and those of us who transmit to you. We are pleased that you take notes of our transmissions and invite you to study and compare them with the notes from other groups. Do not be disturbed that one of us seems to be sending messages simultaneously to different groups. This is quite possible. The mind is capable of doing several things at once, if properly trained. As I speak to you, I am working before a huge table of charts.

"Some of you in this group may want to experiment with automatic writing, but pay particular heed to what you get. Believe nothing nor do nothing that will be harmful to yourself or others. Do not try to exploit your interest in us for financial rewards or you will be cheating yourselves of the great abilities that can be yours."

At first glance, the information allegedly received by this group, another like it in Beverly Hills, and yet another in the San Fernando Valley, might sound amazingly like advice from a good book on self-help. Some of the material, frankly suggesting the possibilities of reincarnation and cosmic consciousness, sounds like Rosicrucianism and Theosophy rolled into one, but the point is repeated over and over again, the space people come in peace. They will not be able to contact us en masse or in person for quite some time. We must assure them of our ability to get along well with one another, we must study, we must learn, we must be able to accept things which our minds have no way of assimilating yet.

Some of the study groups have been warned about such diverse matters as charging money for coffee ("If you cannot afford to serve coffee, then do without it."), wearing metal on the body ("Rings often tend to interfere with natural magnetism."), introducing new members to the group ("Do not be too aggressive. Let the individual ask you if you are interested in life on other planets or the possibility of contacting other beings."), and making radical changes in a way of life ("We are not out to become your foster parents and we cannot help you to change personal situations you do not like. We hope to show you the merits and benefits of a way of thinking that will help you in your spiritual advancement, but we do not expect that you will pull up your roots and take to the hills in fear of cataclysm. This is your world. You must live in it, grow in it, and work in it if you are ever to see us or our worlds.").

If there should be some nuclear destruction, they will make

133

reasonable attempts to rescue as many of us as possible, but even so, physical death is not the ultimate end of the spiritual being. There are more possibilities and potentialities.

These study groups sprang up more or less simultaneously with the publicity given to George Van Tassel, but so far as many of the participants in them are concerned, Van Tassel is far removed from their consideration and not likely to be mentioned for months on end.

A UFO group in Pacific Palisades is completely unaware of the Lynwood group and, when given a description of the activities, tended to scoff, "Oh, that sounds a bit on the religious side. We're realists here. We're interested in seeing to it that people are convinced UFOs are real and that there has been a serious conspiracy to keep the truth from the public."

It would seem that the study groups who are in contact with space people could put forth their questions and suggestions in a practical way, getting practical results and actual proof that would stand up in a scientific inquiry. But they are reminded that physical proof is not the issue to those who truly want to advance.

This state of affairs could last just so long before splinter groups began to form. Already, many of the persons who attended the more spiritual-sounding UFO groups have dropped out or moved over to more militant groups, which simply gather data about new sightings and spend their time trying to catch sight of a UFO of their own.

Each new batch of sightings causes some dropouts to return to the fold, as if in anticipation of something big. But this factor leaves many UFO study groups at a curious crossroads. Many of the "dropouts" are convinced that they need not return because they have been given the basic fundamentals of an education that they may pursue by themselves, either through reading or much smaller discussions. The reading ranges from Isaac Asimov's *The New Intelligent Man's Guide to Science* to *Ohaspe*, a cosmological and metaphysical treatise on the nature of the universe, from stories of mysterious underground cities and of lost continents to pamphlets on RNA and DNA, the two new genetic discoveries that have given entirely new depth and dimension to our concept of life.

While this attempt to reconcile the scientific with the metaphysical continues, other groups become more militant and are hoping to pressure appropriate governmental agencies into revealing all they know about the UFO phenomena to date. In a sense, even the most rabid of UFO fans and groups have one thing in common with the most conservative investigator on Project Bluebook; they both want to see a physical specimen, a body, a wreckage, or some tangible proof that the UFO is not a will-o'-the-wisp.

Each month, hundreds of UFO publications are issued in addition to the coverage given the subject by the mass market magazines. One such publication is *Probe* a bimonthly in Woonsocket, R.I. In twenty pages, *Probe* manages to give reports on new sightings, suggest that there is enlightenment to come in studying the ways of space people, take a sharp knock at some of the foes of the movement, review some related books, and maintain a pre-1947 sighting log. *Probe* has correspondents in twenty states, all of whom send in material and clippings from local newspapers.

From Amherst, Wisc., Ray Palmer, a veteran writer and editor of science fiction, puts out *Flying Saucers,* a lively bimonthly crammed with UFO lore and dedicated to the proposition that UFOs are flying saucers and that flying saucers are a matter of fact. Even Dr. Menzel attests to the quality of the factual accounts in this magazine which is not connected with any club or pro-UFO organization.

UFO comes out of Virginia, and there are at least five other publications bearing the name *UFO* or *UFOs Are Real*. They are mimeographed and range from ten legal-sized sheets to sixteen. Their circulation must be limited and, although done in legible typing, strongly suggest they are labors involving more love than any profit. Favorite targets are the U.S. Air Force, scientists, skeptics, and people who will not take a stand.

These publications, including the *APRO Bulletin, Cosmic Researcher, Interplanetary News Service, Saucerian Bulletin, CRIFO Orbit,* and the *UFO Critical Bulletin* represent a curious and lively kind of special-interest journalism, where each new event is greeted with hoopla and enthusiasm.

Such publications as *Fate* magazine find UFOs excellent copy and may be said to carry one or more UFO items per month. Even *The Cosmic Star, The New Cosmic Star,* and *Chimes,* which are quite catholic in their occult, metaphysical, and stories-of-the-unusual tastes, manage to feature a good deal of UFO material, and a visit to most used book stores will generally bring forth some colorful surprises of related or unrelated interest. Just for example, while libraries and the well-known *Books in Print* don't mention the fact, and neither, apparently, does the author, nevertheless, Major Donald E. Keyhoe's interest in his pre-UFO days was aviator Charles Lindbergh.

Many of the civilian UFO study groups put out publications of some sort on a more or less regular basis. Some of these groups are: Borderland Sciences Research Associates, Interplanetary Intelligence of Unidentified Flying Objects,

Intercontinental Aerial Research Foundation, UFO Research Committee, Waukegan, Ill., Contact Group, Saucer Investigative Research Organization, World Society of the Flying Saucer, Civilian Research on Interplanetary Flying Objects, the National Investigations Committee on Aerial Phenomena, and, the oldest of the lot, the APRO, headed by Mrs. Coral Lorenzen.

As is the case with some of the unnamed study groups, some of the civilian organizations mentioned above have definite standards of membership. Contactees, for instance, are not particularly encouraged in NICAP, although Dan Fry is a member of that group. Membership is theoretically opened to any person with a sincere interest in UFOs and in militating for a major investigation, that is, if he is not a member of the Communist party. The April–May 1960 issue of *UFO Investigator,* the NICAP publication, tells of a group of contactees who were dropped from membership for failure to tell the council of their history in advance of joining.

The most noteworthy noncivilian investigating group is, of course, Project Bluebook, headed by the U.S. Air Force, under the direction of Major Hector Quintanilla, Jr. With headquarters at Wright-Patterson Air Force Base in Dayton, Ohio, Project Bluebook has received an amazing assortment of items and objects purporting to be parts of UFOs or of some extraterrestrial origin. "We're not trying to hold anything back," Major Quintanilla says, implying that the samples of objects he's seen and investigated to date always turn out to be of a decidedly earthly origin. However, "We accept every report as valid unless there is evidence to substantiate a report as a hoax."

Working in direct conjunction with Project Bluebook is Dr. Allen Hynek, members of the Air Force with special technical training, whose duty it is to investigate and analyze UFO reports; a panel of military and civilian experts in all branches of science, massive laboratory facilities, meteorological records of the U.S. Weather Bureau, and civilian laboratories which are under government contract to carry out special work for the Air Force.

Perhaps it is the very massiveness of this organization that seems to enrage so many individuals and civilian groups. Past performances show that Project Bluebook has been caught persisting in rather thin stories and many groups are willing to forgive and forget the past. But they cannot understand why more conclusive evidence has not been presented by the organization with the best potential in the world for discovering the truth.

"The Air Force would have a lot of technical knowledge to gain from examining a real UFO," Major Quintanilla says, implying directly that it has not already done so.

"The Air Force is still holding back," another group will counter, implying directly that the Air Force has already done so.

And the battle starts all over again, while both sides look eagerly to the skies, where some startling discoveries and theories are being made.

CHAPTER ELEVEN

Intelligent Life on Other Planets

The reports of several persons that they were contacted by a variety of different, humanoid-appearing people from other planets met with more snickers of amusement or embarrassment, depending on the case, than they met with scientific interest. And one of the great ironies is that one of the more preposterous and patently fraudulent claims of extraterrestrial contact helped to raise some of the most intelligent issues.

The case involved W. O. Schmidt, a Nebraska grain buyer, who encountered, or so he said, a spacecraft operated by natives of the planet Saturn. So well did Schmidt ingratiate himself with these visitors that he was taken on several flights, including visits to the Arctic Circle, below the Bering Straits, where he saw Russian suboceanic missile emplacements; to the North Pole; and a memorable trip to the Great Pyramid of Giza in Egypt. It was here that Schmidt was shown a secret room in the pyramid, a room in which he was shown three objects of great significance: a dusty old flying saucer, a huge wooden cross, and a crown of thorns. The explanation was that a Saturnian had attempted a mission on earth nearly two thousand years ago and had met with some great measure of success.

Schmidt's trips with his Saturnian friends made him a great

favorite at lectures and UFO discussion groups, a fact he took great advantage of by collecting meals and fees. But it was the saucer trip over a quartz mine in California that gave Schmidt the best idea of all, and in no time he was telling people of the miraculous mine pointed out to him by his friends from Saturn. There was no question about it, this particular grade of quartz was recognized by the Saturnians as having cancer-curing properties.

After a time, some of the people to whom Schmidt talked of this marvelous mine prevailed upon him to allow them to purchase shares. This was the reason Schmidt found himself on trial. He had neglected to keep track of the number of shares he sold in the mine. And even if he had, it wouldn't have mattered; the mine belonged to someone else.

One of the expert witnesses brought in by the prosecuting attorney in the case was Dr. Carl Sagan, an astronomer and astrophysicist. Playing the part of an amused straightman in a comedy of absurdity, the district attorney asked Dr. Sagan for his conclusions on the possibility of human or human-like beings on Saturn.

Dr. Sagan said the chances were there, but they were slim chances. It would be amazing if four and a half billions' years of separate and independent biological evolution on both planets could produce similar results. Besides, the mass of Saturn was 17 per cent greater than on earth, making it more likely that a living being from Saturn would be more squat than we of earth.

This would seem to have wrapped up the matter for Schmidt, but his defense attorney was not finished. In a matter of a few minutes, the attorney had the jury rattled and had planted a seed of curiosity in Dr. Sagan's mind. Weren't we assuming without evidence that the same laws that exist for physical properties on earth must hold true for Saturn? the attorney asked.

Earlier, Dr. Sagan had testified that the parts of Saturn which are accessible to our telescopes are probably several hundred degrees below zero. Now, the defense attorney moved in. If the temperature of earth were computed from the same set of circumstances, say from the tops of our cloud layers, what would the temperature of earth be estimated at? Probably, Dr. Sagan replied, at around minus sixty or seventy degrees Fahrenheit.

No, this stratagem did not win an acquittal for Schmidt. He was convicted and sentenced. And no, the attorney's clever questions did not cause any serious reevaluation of the laws of physics or astronomy. But they did cause a rather brilliant man to examine his thinking and strengthen his ardent hope and thesis that intelligent life could exist on other planets. At least, Sagan is dedicated to doing what he can to find out, one way or the other.

Many scientists are involved in a similar form of study, and one important reason why they and men like Dr. Menzel seem so cautious is because of the way some of them have been quoted out of context or have had additional meanings written into their statements for the dramatic effectiveness of a good story. An example is the recent and not exactly well-founded assumption that the 1965 Mariner IV spacecraft has proved Mars to be dead, without the possibility of life.

The fact is that Mariner IV was not designed to give information that could lead to such a direct assumption. And, turning the tables again as the defense attorney did with Dr. Sagan, if the Mariner IV of 1965 were fired from Mars to earth, it could just as easily have relayed information that might lead to the conclusion that life on this planet was impossible. The designers of Mariner IV were at pains to point out that the mission of their craft did not demonstrate the possibility of life on Mars, nor did it in any way preclude the possibility.

Loren Eiseley, who was quoted in the previous chapter, has independently reached the same conclusion as Dr. Sagan: any life we find on other planets and in other systems is very unlikely to resemble our own. Too many variables went into our own evolution for us to expect a duplication or approximation of us.

This does not rule out the possibility of the very humanlike persons reportedly seen by Adamski and others, nor does it disprove once and for all A-lan's contention of descent from ancient persons who once inhabited our planet. But let's look at it this way, the information contained in a single human sperm cell is equivalent to 133 volumes of *Webster's Third New International Dictionary*. That includes the size of the volume, the thinness of paper, and the number of entries. At present, we are forced by sheer weight of numbers to conclude that the possibilities of such an intensive duplication are rather limited.

Nevertheless, the assumption that there is life out in the vast reaches of space is one that is supported with cautious optimism by many scientists who study the skies. What are some of the findings that cause us to think of the possibilities of life on other worlds?

One has to do with the number of radio signals received from galactic sources during the past forty years. There are no apparent explanations to these signals yet, but speculation is running high that they might be some intelligent sort of transmission, since their characteristics do not suggest a mere reflection of galactic noise.

Another has to do with observations made on the planet Mars. Some of the inferences which can be rather safely drawn about Mars definitely do not preclude the possibility of life on this planet, a place where man is almost certain to walk within the next twenty years.

Dr. Lewis Kaplan of California Institute of Technology's Jet Propulsion Laboratory in Pasadena made a recent report that a project on which he collaborated with two French astronomers gives even stronger inferences than ever before that some form of life does exist on Mars.

Working with Pierre and Janine Connes, Dr. Kaplan said new observations now suggest the presence of methane and methanelike materials on Mars. Methane is a natural gas. It is used popularly on earth as a fuel for heaters, for cooking, and for firing industrial boilers. Its presence in earthly atmosphere comes as the result of the activity of living creatures. It is usually associated with the presence of hydrogen atoms, an important enough discovery in itself since it was previously believed that Mars was too small to hold hydrogen atoms in its atmosphere. Both hydrogen and methane are connected with living organisms and hydrogen, particularly, is held to be the key to the development of higher life forms.

While the presence of these two elements in quantity does not guarantee the presence of life on Mars, it is regarded as an argument against the detractors of the life on Mars theory and is generally held to be a cause for optimism.

The most obvious and common argument used to support life on this planet is the system of so-called canals. Although not exactly precise in definition, the word canal is not inaccurate, either. The Italian astronomer who first noted and identified this network called them *canalli,* which could just as easily be called grooves. Each Spring (a Martian Spring) when the polar caps melt, a darkening is seen along the equatorial regions. The darkening spreads out near the canals or grooves and gives us the impression that the water may be used for irrigation purposes.

Our scientists can agree that Mars has very little water, but many argue that most of the water there would tend to stay and not vaporize.

The fact that almost no radio waves come from Mars tends, on the surface, to imply that there may be no life on Mars, but this is only a brief consideration. If the Martians were only fifty years behind us in progress, they would have no radio. If they were fifty years ahead of us, however, this might mean they had used electromagnetic forces as a more efficient means of transmission, effectively keeping their transmissions from being eavesdropped upon.

If we turn the tables for a moment and assume the Martians are attempting to discover whether or not intelligent life exists on earth, we have another story. Surprisingly enough, the Martians have only two good clues to go on, one is the pattern of vegetation on this planet, the other is the matter of radio waves. Each time the continents of North America and Europe are turned toward Mars, a tremendous frequency of radio waves are beamed in their direction, enough to convince them that a great deal is artificial and, thus, produced by intelligent life. Yet these are the only two ways Martians could be at all sure and even then, there would be some heated debate among their scientists.

Heated is a good word, because it applies to another conclusion the Martians might make about us. Using a spectroscope to measure Earth, the Martians might possibly conclude that the quantities of oxygen and water on Earth are huge, especially when compared to the contents of Mars. This would cause them to think of our temperatures as being unbearably hot, and it is quite likely that they would note the absence of ultraviolet light on our surface. All these are factors which would, from their point of view, cause them to abandon any hope of finding life on this planet.

Turning the tables like this does not, of course, prove that there is life on Mars, it merely opens up some interesting conjecture and gives us another way of being more optimistic when we crib from Mark Twain to say that reports of no life on the planet Mars are still exaggerated.

Besides, if we are capable of sending out as sophisticated a piece of machinery as the Mariner IV, if we are reasonably sure in advance of the probable success of the devices already completed for gathering soil samples and photographs from the planet Mars, it does not take very much imagination to accept flying saucers if we just give the Martians an edge in progress of fifty years.

There are already hundreds of billions of known worlds in the universe, and we have strong reasons for believing that the same basic elements which comprise our earth also comprise, in different proportions, other worlds. If the hydrogen atom could evolve, as it did here, to result in the human brain structure, the chances of it developing along similar lines to form something similar to the brain on other worlds are excellent.

Although listening devices have been tuned in on other stars, and some degree of study has been made, three of our closest neighbors have been the closest source of inspection with regard to discovering the possibility of life. These are our moon, Mars, and Venus. Because it is generally seen covered by clouds, we know less about Venus than we would like to, certainly less than we know about the moon or Mars.

At this point in our development, and based on what we know to date, it is safer to conclude that there is no life on the moon than it is safe to make the same conclusion about Mars. In fact, an encouraging statement on those lines comes from Dr. William Pickering of the Jet Propulsion Laboratories at the California Institute of Technology. Dr. Pickering says there are many similarities between the planets Earth and Mars, they are both seasonal, they both have polar caps, they both tilt at approximately the same axis, they are of an approximate size. "It is feasible from what we know about life on Earth," he says, "that life could exist on Mars."

Because they are comparatively close—eleven light-years away—and because we think they are likely to have habitable planets, the stars Epsilon Eridani and Tau Ceti have been the source of listening operations on a limited scale. The results caused the then director of the National Radio Astronomy Observatory to conclude that "it was pretty dull on Epsilon Eridani and Tau Ceti eleven years ago." And all persons concerned with the project agree that it would have been nearly miraculous if the approximately two hundred hours spent in monitoring would have produced immediate results. The two stars have not been abandoned as being a good potential of life-bearing planets.

The distance between earth and other galaxies may be staggering. Since we know there are hundreds of billions of stars and hundreds of billions of planets in the universe, our most logical approach is to investigate those as close to us as possible, but while we await the results of these "neighbors," there must also be some attention paid to those systems which may be hundreds and possibly thousands of light-years away. Such a contact would be truly amazing and miraculous. Imagine the possibility of hearing intelligent signals from a planet that had developed a technical civilization over a thousand years ago . . . or even before our earth became habitable.

Working in collaboration with Dr. Sagan, a noted Russian astronomer named Iosef Shklovskii concludes that about one billion planets are populated with their own varieties of living organisms. He says that on some of these planets life may well have existed for such long periods of time that intelligent life forms could have evolved, and, in turn, could have produced technical civilizations. This is particularly encouraging to our argument when we consider that earth was billions of years old before the development of intelligent life.

Of primary importance, according to Dr. Shklovskii, is the need for greater understanding of the processes leading to evolution of intelligence and technical civilizations. In the meantime, he is content to conclude that the rise of intelligent life in a universe filled with planetary systems seems to be a likely phenomenon.

One of the huge problems inherent in contact with other planets seems to be that of distance and time. Distance is measured astronomically in at least two basic ways. One of these is the AU or astronomical unit or 93 million miles, the distance between the sun and our planet. The more familiar way is the light-year, the distance traveled by light in one earth year.

If UFOs are truly interplanetary and some of the information passed on to the contactees may be believed at all, there is a method of transportation and communication that moves more quickly than the speed of light. And if there is not, we're in trouble. A trip to Epsilon Eridani and Tau Ceti would take eleven years each way, assuming that fueling could be arranged. Communication would also take as long to these stars, and there is the distinct possibility that messages sent beyond a hundred or so light years distance could become very weak unless the tuning was exquisitely accurate.

Even if this is the only method of communication between worlds, it is possible that we could send and exchange plans for building models of cities, aircraft, scientific devices, and even the genetic constructions of extraterrestrial organisms. As rewarding as such contact would be, it is, at best, a frustrating concept. Imagine having to wait out the intervening years once a contact had been established. And imagine trying to recruit volunteers for voyages that would age a man from twenty to forty years on a single trip. Science seems to have caught up with science fiction in two interesting proposals, in the event that the speed of light is, as many scientists claim, a limiting factor.

The two most tangible-sounding proposals from our scientists now have to do with inhibiting human metabolic activities and with placing humans in frozen states of suspended animation. If this seems too much to bear, don't worry, no one has yet tried a human guinea pig; and besides, attention is being given quite seriously to the theory of relativity. Called time dilation, the theory, in its simplest terms, means that travel at high speeds out in space would be very slow when measured in comparison with the passage of time here on Earth. Dr. Sagan explains it this way: "As the passengers would travel over immense distances of thousands of light years or more at relativistic velocities, they would become only slightly older. This phenomenon of relativistic time dilation is a specific consequence of the theory of special relativity formulated by Albert Einstein, a theory whose other applications have been repeatedly verified."

Aboard a spacecraft moving at relativistic speeds, the clocks would move more slowly than the clocks on earth, the hearts

of any passengers would beat more slowly, and their awareness of the passage of time would be greatly slowed down.

For the sake of a few past arguments, we've turned a few
tables on some information we've discussed, so why not once
more? In this case, why not turn the tables in favor of spacecraft traveling to Earth from Mars, Venus, or the moon? If the
moon is not habitable, it is still a convenient stopping-off
place, and if Venus and Mars are inhabited, some of the
apparent speeds of the UFOs discussed earlier would certainly
give them the necessary velocity to escape the atmospheres of
these worlds and make the trip to Earth.

We've made quite a jump from scientists who think UFOs
are social phenomena, figments of the imagination, or merely
occurrences we cannot yet explain to the scientists who are
actively postulating the possibilities. The Soviet ethnologist
M. M. Agrest has been working on a hypothesis that makes
some of the Biblical references we surveyed in Chapter
Three. Although not actively influenced by Morris K. Jessup,
Agrest is certainly using another approach to taking the Bible
literally. In 1959, Agrest said he had postulated that repre-
sentatives from extraterrestrial civilizations have visited our
planet. His means of doing so was to check carefully through
the legends and myths of peoples of the Earth, looking for
traces of useful arts and sciences which might be reflected in
stories, both written and verbal, handed down from generation to generation. Paying close attention to the arrival and
departure of aliens from the sky and then back into the sky,
Agrest drew some startling conclusions, none of which he can
prove; but, like some of the more recent UFO sightings, many
of which he cannot disprove.

Of particular significance to Agrest was the Biblical description of the destruction of Sodom and Gomorrah, which

reminded him of a nuclear explosion as it might have been reported through the eyes of a contemporary observer. There is also some reason for thinking of the two cities as possible population centers on the two lost continents of Atlantis and Mu.

A great deal of speculation arose when Henri Lhote discovered on the cliffs overlooking the Sahara Desert the fresco of a Martian, complete with space suit, and a hole in the helmet for one eye, directly in the center. After more investigation, it was discovered that a distant tribe had, at one time, used a headmask and costume representing the figure on the fresco. This helmet and costume was used as a part of a ritual dance. And, as far back as the ritual dance can be traced, there is no apparent indication of an extraterrestrial landing. But the matter may not end here. This tribe did not keep written records; a great deal of its information was passed along verbally and in a few pictures. So there really isn't proof that M. Lhote's discovery is not quite significant and quite Martian.

Other drawings, frescoes, and engravings exist which may reflect only a fanciful guess on the part of some civilizations, or they may be accurate reflections of a past knowledge that was truly amazing. For instance, some ancient art clearly shows excellent maps of the heavens in which nine planets revolve merrily about our sun while other contemporary drawings and etchings show only five or six.

Ancient languages, when examined, show word meanings and derivations for which no possible explanations exist, that is, unless you accept the notion that these past civilizations were given highly specialized information, not apparently available to anyone else on earth, by a person or persons who were not from this earth.

Agrest discovered an apocryphal book, *The Slavonic Enoch*, which caused him more than momentary interest. To all apparent intents, this book seems to be an account of the visit from extraterrestrial cosmonauts and their taking as their guest a somewhat bewildered and amazed earthling to their planet. There are two or three points against this work being taken more seriously than it is, but it does raise some interesting doubts.

In general, the myths and legends of ancient alleged contacts by extraterrestrials are awkward, crude, inaccurate, and yet filled with a definite sincerity and a common basis of probability. Interestingly enough, some of the more modern versions of accounts written by contactees bear marked similarities. Perhaps because of their crudeness and almost naïve approach, they tend to embarrass government scientists and civilian UFO groups who are bent on gaining some respect. But they make for interesting reading, they intrigue many scientists who are convinced of life on other planets, and they should form some of the background of any beginner interested in the potentials of UFOs.

Another related topic shows the possibility of reality for the UFOs. This topic is what we think we can do out in space right now and in the not-too-distant future. When you hear of the Mark III Gulliver being sent aloft, cross your fingers. If the Mark III Gulliver is successful, it will send detailed analyses of soil, rock, plant, and small animal life back to earth. If we reach Venus and discover, underneath all those clouds and mists, that the planet is not inhabited, Dr. Carl Sagan thinks he can do something about it; he thinks he can perform operations which would make that planet habitable by us.

These are mere drops in the cosmic bucket. A Russian,

Constantin Tsiolkovskii, came up with an idea for rebuilding our solar system. His work, not so farfetched as it may sound, directly anticipated the discovery and building of the solar battery, one of the great power sources of our space probes today. This imaginative thinker was working in 1895. But two modern Americans, completely unaware of Tsiolkovskii, have come up with similar conclusions. In essence, their proposal would be the harnessing of asteroids and solar power to restructure the solar system and make extensive colonization possible, particularly on the moon. Although these plans would take a few hundred years, once the technical knowledge began with the basic operations, the details would become easier. This is no longer a wild dream. Talk about population explosion, such a plan, when implemented, would make room for the present population of the world plus an additional 1,000,000,000,000,000 persons.

In Chapter Six, we gave some examination to the scientists and laymen who felt that UFOs were not possible. In this chapter we've seen some traces of the kinds of theories and actual work some of the very scientists who write off UFOs are now engaged with. It becomes an entirely different matter when we see how these men extrapolate, theorize, and work toward such positive, amazing goals.

In the light of our own accomplishments and expectations for the future, it becomes relatively simple to think seriously of other worlds and other scientists already having made sufficient progress in their work to develop craft which can fly through space—large, cigar-shaped craft which contain smaller, saucerlike craft which probe the atmosphere about Earth, measuring, watching, and investigating.

Each year, as we send more probe vehicles out into space, we are moving one more step along the way of advertising our presence to our neighbors—whomever they might be—out in space. We've had about fifty years of sending out intelligible radio waves, nearly twenty years of sending out television waves, and about that much time in sending out the telltale traces of our familiarity with some aspects of atomic fission. Some of the many scientific projects on the drawing boards and in the prototype stages are really more amazing and more difficult for us to accept than the concept of the UFO being a real entity, yet we still find it convenient to accept the one and reject the possibility of the other.

Past UFO sightings have been written off as: flocks of birds, reflections of sunlight on clouds, organisms, fireflies, planets, unusual light patterns, balloons, artificial earth satellites, aircraft seen in uncommon weather conditions, refracted light, and the Aurora Borealis. Perhaps some of them are these things. But that leaves the balance, the unaccounted for UFOs, the ones seen at close range by many persons who could not be shaken in their stories. The odds in favor of UFOs being real, dimensional spacecraft suddenly assume an intriguing and compelling significance that we may still choose to ignore, but not for much longer.

CHAPTER TWELVE

If You See a UFO

You are likely to spot a UFO at any time of the day, in any part of the country. The chances are that you will not have a pair of binoculars or a telescope handy, and the odds are a little less than even that you will have a camera to photograph what you do see. Even then, the chance of your getting one or more discernible pictures is about one in ten. Nervousness, eagerness, and anxiety will play a part in how you act and what you do under these circumstances.

There are very few hard-and-fast rules for you to follow, but the most important thing of all, do not panic. If you do, your observation is likely to be less memorable and less helpful. Perhaps if you are able to keep a few rules and approaches in mind, you will have so much to do that there won't be time for panic.

Try to get witnesses, the more, the better.

If you are driving an automobile when you make your sighting, pull over to the side of the road at the earliest safe moment and get out of the car. This will help eliminate the possibility that what you see is a reflection or refraction.

Note the time as best you can. Try to get a good reading on the time your UFO was first seen and the time when it was no longer in view.

Try to pinpoint the UFO in relation to a fixed object. For instance, if you see a UFO in an area where there are trees, try to estimate the height of the UFO over one particular tree. The easiest way to do this is with your hand. Sighting along the bottom of your hand, line your hand up with the top of the tree. Even if you are able to estimate that your UFO was hovering "two handwidths" above the tree, an investigator will be able to compute the altitude if he knows the approximate spot where you stood when you made your sighting. If you're out of doors, you can make some distinctive marking with your foot in grass, dirt, or gravel. If you happen to be on pavement or sidewalk, try to measure the height from a fixed place such as a fire hydrant, curbing, etc. Or merely drop a coin at the approximate spot where you are standing.

Try to find something in your pocket or nearby that you can use to help measure relative size. For instance, your UFO might be the size of a quarter, held at arm's length.

If the UFO begins to move, try to make an approximation of the amount of time it takes to pass between two fixed points. Anything may serve as a useful reference point here. UFOs have been timed between two distant mountain peaks, between a tree and a house, between a particular building and another, etc. This is all good information for professional investigators who can convert your fixed points into actual distances and arrive at a close approximation.

If you have a camera, make sure you do not allow your excitement to cause you to shake. Don't be in too much of a hurry. One photograph with good, sharp details is better than six blurred, out-of-focus shots. When you get the opportunity to photograph a UFO, attempt to get some other object into the photo for purposes of relative size, for shadows, etc. This will make it less likely that your picture is suspected of being a hoax. Get as much of the picture as you can. This means, try to get in unusual shadows or exhaust patterns or any disturbances the UFO may be causing on the ground. The obvious swirl of dust under one UFO photo has done more to insure its acceptance as real than any other single factor. Once you think you have shot your UFO in relationship to its locale, then you can concentrate on additional pictures of details, trying for as many different angles as possible.

If it becomes apparent to you that the UFO you have seen is landing, wait for a chance to get it completely at rest. If it appears to you that the UFO contains living persons, proceed with optimistic caution. Approach slowly, make no sudden or threatening movements, and do your best to prepare yourself for an attempt at telepathic communication. Even if your visitors are not capable of communicating with you by telepathy, it will certainly assist you to maintain your poise by thinking strongly that you are as friendly and curious as possible.

Remember that the contact may be just as exciting for your visitor as it is for you. If you attempt to take photos of these possible visitors, do so in a way that does not suggest to them that your camera may be a weapon.

If you are in a situation where a UFO—large enough to be manned or merely a small automatic device—seems to be chasing you or moving at you, do the sensible thing and head for cover, but do not conclude that you are being attacked until you have definite, sufficient reason to believe this. Head for whatever cover is closest at hand, but try to make it obvious, at least at first, that you are present. There have been incidents where UFOs appeared to give chase or approach at close range, but nothing they have done to date seems to justify the conclusion of a hostile intent.

Be cooperative as soon as you can. As much as you want information, so will your visitor, and the more natural you are able to act, the more natural your visitor will be able to be. There are possibilities that such an alien visitor might not look exactly human. No matter how repugnant this person might seem to you, do your best to keep in mind how important this contact might be and how necessary it is for you to assume the role of a gracious host. Out in the midst of a desert, face-to-face with a strange-looking alien, this may seem like an absurd suggestion, but it is important to convey a friendly interest.

If possible, make some effort to exchange some articles of property. A watch, pencil, ballpoint pen, even a picture, offered as a gift may bring in exchange even more emphatic proof of interplanetary flight and evidence of other civilizations than ours. Some scientists may have devoted ten years to digging through old ruins for an object of less significance than what you might be given as a trade.

Do your best to suggest further contact now and in the future.

As soon as your contact is ended, make every effort to identify the exact site of your sighting or contact.

The chances of your film being given official recognition and acceptance are greater if you allow the Air Force investigators to remove the exposed film from your camera. If you have the film processed yourself, make sure the persons doing the processing know what they have and can make statements to the effect that the film came directly from your camera.

At the earliest possible moment, write down or dictate into a tape recorder the details of your sighting while it is still fresh in your mind. Forget about the unnecessary detail and stick to what you saw. Describe it in the best and most complete terms possible, then attempt to make a drawing of it. Forget all about winning free art courses, get the details down on paper and try to give the proper proportions as best you can.

If you are worried about publicity or what people will think of you, you are within your rights to say nothing to newspapers or other media until you have contacted an investigating agency and given over your material.

Without any intended prejudices, it is suggested that the reports be sent either to Project Bluebook headquarters at Wright-Patterson Air Force Base, Dayton, Ohio, or to the University of Colorado. From all indications, these two organizations have the best means of evaluating all the data you supply. But there is nothing to prevent you from sending your reports elsewhere if you desire.

It is important to remember the complaints of many scientists and investigators that observers do not always see what they think they are seeing. If you have the time to investigate your sighting closely, some simple, logical explanation may present itself to you. In all fairness, you should consider the possibility of mirage, optical illusion, reflection, weather conditions, etc. If you are still convinced that you have truly seen a UFO, then by all means, make your report.

It is only human to want to share such a momentous experience with others, and if the UFO you saw was witnessed by other observers, the chances are that you will be even more eager to stand up and be counted as a sighter of UFOs. It is also perfectly natural for you to consider writing your story for a magazine or trying to make a book of it, or carrying your impressions to groups and meetings. But remember this, the more dignity you lend to your experience, the more reason others will have to believe in you and UFOs.